Praise for *Hurt Healer*:

"Through the pages of his life story Tony Nolan challenges and encourages us to reach out fearlessly and let the hurting see God in us. *Hurt Healer* compassionately and practically gives you the goods to pull it off right now!" —TobyMac, recording artist; author, *City on Our Knees*

"Tony masterfully uses the ancient parable of the Good Samaritan and his own modern day life story to prove that God was, and still is, the ultimate hurt healer. Part exposition, part memoir, part devotional, and all worth reading." —David Nasser, author, *Jumping through Fires*

"The church is in desperate need of the truths that Tony has so beautifully shared in the pages of *Hurt Healer*. With each chapter I began to get more and more excited about the journey that God has me on to love those around me, and yet at the same time so convicted about my own love walk. Tony has an amazing gift in being able to take Bible stories we have heard countless times and make them come alive. This book helps us to freely give as we've so freely received." —Alyssa Barlow, BarlowGirl

"Tony Nolan is one of my greatest friends. He loves Jesus with a passion like no one else I know. He loves his family as Christ loves the church. And he wakes up in the morning with a lost world on his heart. You will see his heart for Jesus and people as you read *Hurt Healer*. And you will be challenged to reach the world one person at a time!" —Mark Hall, Casting Crowns

"Tony Nolan shares with us his own personal, painful experiences and reveals to us the Healer, Jesus Christ, who knows no limits in healing those hurts. Tony challenges us to share this Healer with those who don't know him, and he confronts us with the fact that the Healer expects us to be his soothing salve." —Sonny Perdue, governor, State of Georgia

"Tony understands the way in and the way out of hurt. Trust what he says, take his advice, and let him lead you into a life of hope in Christ." —Brandon Heath, recording artist

"Tony Nolan truly has an ear for what God is saying to young people in this generation. Through this book, *Hurt Healer*, I believe God will empower Tony's voice to impact many others through the life saving message of Jesus Christ. You will appreciate Tony's authenticity as he shares from his personal experiences. And you will enjoy his storytelling ability as he retells biblical narratives in a fresh and engaging way." —Chip Rogers, majority leader, Georgia Senate

Praise for Tony Nolan:

"We were the first guys to use Tony Nolan and we knew everybody else would want him. He is humble, animated, outta control and speaks from his heart in twenty-seven flavors. He has a message, and people love to hear it from him." —Lanny Donoho, Big Cheese of Catalyst Conferences; founder of Big Stuf Student Camps

"Tony Nolan is a one-of-a-kind speaker and minister whose heart is for the lost. He has a way of relating to hurting people that is honest, heartfelt, and real. I'm so grateful to know him and his family personally and to have watched him deliver the gospel night after night with the same enthusiasm on several tours. Read this book!" —Francesca Battistelli, recording artist

"Tony Nolan is one of the most gifted gospel communicators I have heard in a long time. He is direct, clear, humorous, and effective!" —Ronnie Floyd, lead pastor, The Church at Pinnacle Hills

"Tony Nolan and his family were awesome to partner with in ministry! Tony's passion and zeal to be open and real with people is a breath of fresh air today. No 'going through the motions'; no sugarcoated gospel about giving only 'part' of your life to Jesus; and best of all, no apologies! Just straight up radical Christianity." —John Cooper, Skillet

"Tony is a great communicator and a great encourager to all those he is around. He's a blessing and a faith builder to all he speaks to." —Robby Shaffer, MercyMe

"It has been an honor and privilege to get to know and work with Tony Nolan. The love of Jesus truly reflects though his life. In the last three consecutive years we invited Tony to speak at our Christian Family Day at the Ballpark and we saw an amazing harvest for God's glory!" —Albert and Deidre Pujols, The Pujols Foundation

"Tony has been with us two times and we had a great harvest of souls. He has an amazing gift of preaching the gospel and 'drawing the net.' When Tony Nolan preaches the gospel, the altar will be filled with people of all ages coming to Christ." —Dr. Fred Lowery, pastor of First Bossier and Host of First Word

HURTHEALER

reaching out to a broken world

TONY NOLAN

Ps.147:3

BakerBooks
a division of Baker Publishing Group
Grand Rapids, Michigan

© 2010 by Tony Nolan

Published by Baker Books
a division of Baker Publishing Group
P.O. Box 6287, Grand Rapids, MI 49516-6287
www.bakerbooks.com

Printed in the United States of America

Library of Congress Cataloging-in-Publication Data
Nolan, Tony.
    Hurt healer : reaching out to a broken world / Tony Nolan.
       p.   cm.
    Includes bibliographical references.
    ISBN 978-0-8010-1352-2 (cloth)
    1. Evangelistic work. I. Title.
BV3790.N58 2010
269'.2—dc22   2010014871

10   11   12   13   14   15   16   7   6   5   4   3   2   1

To my wife, Tammy, in profound appreciation
for her willingness to magnify the Lord
with me and exalt his name together

Contents

Foreword

Tony Nolan takes us back not only a few years to his own personal healing, but over 2,000 years to show us how this healing was made possible. After being abandoned by his natural parents, being abused by his adoptive father, and becoming a skeptic, to say the least, Tony found real healing. If anyone understands the culture and its attitude in the twenty-first century, it is one who has been there and done that. Tony offers hope to a generation of desperately hopeless people.

Tony is an enthusiastic guy, and his enthusiasm has been generated by the God who embraced him and radically changed his life. His story is both convincing and enlightening. It will prompt readers to look within and wonder, *Could this possibly happen in my life as well?*

If there was ever a generation or a time in history when people were in need of hope, it is now. This book has the potential to touch a generation not only in America but literally all over the world as we consider that the deepest need, the deepest hurt, and the deepest wounds can only be healed in the person of the Lord Jesus Christ. Tony gives credit where credit is due, and that is in intimacy with Christ.

This generation is waiting for us to show and tell. They are waiting for us to show through emulation what we have proclaimed in our exhortation. They want to know there is someone who genuinely cares and will listen and attempt to understand their personal struggles. Who better understands than one who has been there and knows the misery, hurt, and disappointment that can come from placing our faith in human beings only to realize later that the Creator who made each of us is the one who cares most deeply and understands more correctly how to meet our deepest needs.

I know of no one in this generation who has the platform to speak into the lives of teenagers and young adults with more power and effectiveness than evangelist Tony Nolan. Time and time again I have personally seen God use him to bring radical life change to those with whom he has had the privilege of speaking.

Read this book, pass it on, and watch the hurts be healed through the Healer, God's Son, the Lord Jesus Christ.

Johnny Hunt
Pastor, First Baptist Church
Woodstock, Georgia

Acknowledgments

I'm in Beijing, China, right now to be a hurt healer to a little orphan girl named Fei Fei. In a demonstration of his ferocious love for the abandoned, God led my family to adopt her. While here, I'm feasting on this fascinating country. I just returned from walking on the Great Wall of China—one of the seven wonders of the world. Our guide said it is over 4,000 miles long and took over one million people to build. Some of them died and are actually buried within the wall. It took great sacrifice from great people to build it.

I am well aware that to create something great, it takes great people. I want to thank the people who buried themselves in this work and yet are still alive: My wife, Tammy, and my four children, Christy, Wil, Bradly, and Fei Fei. My assistant, Gayle West. My publishing agents, Kathryn Helmers, Katie Sulkowski, and the rest of the amazing people at Creative Trust. Alice Sullivan and her editing genius skills. Baker Books for taking the risk with a first-time author so that some hurts can be healed. Jesus, who really did give his life, not in building Great Walls, but in tearing them down so all those who hurt can have access to healing.

PART 1

KNOWINGJESUS

1

Know Show

For we are to God the fragrance of Christ among those who are being saved and among those who are perishing.

2 Corinthians 2:15

Christianity sucks!

How could I say such a thing? Well, I didn't. They did.

Who are they?

They are not believers in Jesus. They are obviously put out with the church. They are young, middle-aged, and senior citizens. They have toddlers, toupees, and tattoos. They dance when no one is looking. They drool at the sight and smell of dessert. They nervously chew their fingernails as Ryan Seacrest pauses to reveal the next American Idol. They shed tears at funerals, weddings, and graduations. They feel strongly about issues like abortion, homosexuality, and injustice. They are very human. And what I know about them compels me to make sure we never forget that they exist.

They are the reason I am writing this book, and according to God, they matter . . . a lot!

And because they matter, we must reach out to them.

I want you to know that I was and in a lot of ways still am one of them. I am an unapologetic believer and follower of Jesus Christ. But I haven't always been a believer, nor did I grow up in church. So I get where they're coming from; I understand the negative ideas they have about Christianity. Most of these thoughts about Christians are false, and they faded from my own mind after my conversion. Other beliefs, however, have proven shamefully true.

If they had a MySpace or Facebook profile it would contain a disturbing detail: "turned off to all things Christian." It's hard to conceive people would be bent like that, but they really are. In the book *unChristian*, David Kinnaman and Gabe Lyons indicate that only 3 percent of young people in America have a favorable impression of Jesus as portrayed in the lives of evangelicals. You may not be surprised by this data; neither was I. But what I learned next stunned me. Get this: a high percentage of them said that they had been exposed to Christianity, meaning they had some kind of encounter with something or someone Christian.[1] They visited a church, worked with a Christian, or sat next to a Christian in an English composition class. The point is that they heard or saw something that claimed to be Christian, and their impression about Christianity after the encounter was not very good. If you are a Christian, this data should make you concerned.

These numbers reveal that a spiritual pandemic has infected the church, resulting in a viral decline in church attendance. Consider the statistics provided by Dr. Dan Garland, director of pastoral ministry and church consulting for LifeWay Church. I recently sat in a conference with several hundred other leaders and cringed when he said, "In 1950 over 80 percent of our public school kids went to a Christian church, and now it is down to 4 percent." When I heard this, my heart sank. How can this be? When I was growing up, a few of my friends and family members and I didn't think too highly of Christianity, but I didn't realize that so many people had no interest in God. I didn't realize we are now on the cusp of having a Christless generation in America.

Well, I don't put much faith in statistics. I prefer to touch and feel the evidence of such claims. So I conducted my own little research project. In the last four years I have visited over 153 cities, speaking to well over a million people. Unfortunately, as I have traveled throughout America, I have seen that this negative mindset about Christians really does exist and goes beyond generational lines. Approximately eight out of ten nonreligious people I talked to said Christianity sucks. Some used the term

> **We are now on the cusp of having a Christless generation in America.**

sucks, others said it is dead, several claimed it is irrelevant, and many used words that would make even Bill Maher blush.

How can this be? How can so many people be turned off to this amazing, loving, gracious God that we know? The cause of this great dilemma points to a breakdown between the God that we know and the God that we show. And breakdowns can happen in the most innocent of circumstances.

I heard a story about the parents of a troubled teenager. They desperately needed to connect with their daughter, so they decided to have breakfast with her every morning. The idea was to use that time to connect with her before she connected with the harmful things of the world. Every morning they prepared a simple breakfast of eggs, juice, toast, and jelly. But the piece of toast they gave their daughter was the heel—the hard end of the loaf. This went on for a week until one morning the teenager in disgust picked up the piece of toast, slung it across the room where it stuck to a wall, and screamed, "Is this the extent of your love for me—heel toast? What have I done that makes you hate me so much?"

Dazed, the parents replied, "Honey, we're sorry. The heel of the loaf is our favorite piece."

Do you see it? What happened in that story illustrates our current dilemma in helping people understand Jesus. Innocently enough, we go to church and live our lives loving Jesus. We know how good he is, but it's not getting across to non-Christians. They have tossed back what we have been serving them through our religious lives, screaming their distaste. Will we chalk up their cries as mere outbursts of misbehavior, or will we pause a moment, take a good look at our attempts to connect with them, and make some deep life changes for the sake of reaching out to a broken world?

> **Will we take a good look at our attempts to connect with non-Christians and make some deep life changes for the sake of reaching out to a broken world?**

Remember, I was one of them. I haven't forgotten what it feels like to be broken, enslaved, and hopeless. I have done my share of toast slinging. But a group of believers heard my cry and cared enough to engage me. I am going to unwrap my story throughout this book with high hopes that you will experience a life-changing encounter with God so supernatural that after a non-Christian dines on your version of Jesus, they will be able to declare with the psalmist, "I have tasted and seen that the Lord is good, blessed are those that trust in God!" (see Ps. 34:8).

D E L V E

Who are the people that you know who may have an unfavorable impression of Jesus?

_____

_____

_____

Briefly describe a moment when you had a conversation with someone who had a bad taste in his or her mouth about Christianity.

_____

_____

_____

In this chapter the question is asked: Will we chalk up their cries as mere outbursts of misbehavior, or will we pause a moment, take a good look at our attempts to connect with them, and make some deep life changes for the sake of reaching out to a broken world? Briefly write down your response to that question.

_____

_____

_____

Dear God, hearing that there are many people who are turned off to you, help my ears to hear your heart beat for them as I take this journey through the rest of this book. Amen.

2

More than a Story

For the word of God is living and powerful, and sharper than any two-edged sword, piercing even to the division of soul and spirit, and of joints and marrow, and is a discerner of the thoughts and intents of the heart.

Hebrews 4:12

I grew up in a neighborhood in Jacksonville, Florida, that the locals call Sin City. It has no connection with the luxury and wealth of the famous Sin City of Las Vegas. Instead, it's the antithesis—a ghetto. I'm not talking about a little tag phrase like "that's so ghetto." No, I mean real poverty-stricken, social nightmare ghetto. I grew up among unpredictable drunks, dangerous druggies, and heartless murderers. One night I watched my drunken neighbors knock each other's teeth out in my own front yard. My cousin's boyfriend was shot and killed right up the road from my house. A relative of mine named Oscar had his head shot off by a shotgun in my neighborhood.

Keeping the fear level high was the notorious motorcycle gang called the Outlaws. They were like a pack of ravaging hyenas just a couple of blocks from my house. I recall being terrified by an incident where a rival gang placed a bomb under a rusty old van that was used for grocery shopping. An unsuspecting Outlaw turned the ignition and an explosion rocked several blocks as metal, glass, and body parts shattered windows and covered front yards.

My neighborhood was the kind where you would roll up your windows and lock your doors if you accidently made a wrong turn onto its streets. Kind of like the street an innocent traveler journeyed on in a story found in the Bible.

Although the kind of injustice found in this story occurs every day in our crime-infested cities, this event took place a long time ago on a dusty road in the Middle East. Did you catch what I said? It *took place*. I strongly believe the story we are about to interact with actually happened. Most people think it was only a parable—a story that's made up to help people understand a spiritual principle. But one little word makes that a big problem for me. It's the word *certain*. Keep that word on your radar as you take in this story.

The setting of this passage, Luke 10:25–37, involves a massive gathering of people from all walks of life. Crowds don't usually assemble unless something special is going to take place, so what's the buzz about? What incredible, extraordinary moment is summoning their interest? Standing right in their midst, at the grand center of all their attention, is Jesus from Nazareth. With eyes full of fire and life, the Master of all storytellers says to them,

> A certain man went down from Jerusalem to Jericho, and fell among thieves, who stripped him of his clothing, wounded him, and departed, leaving him half dead. Now by chance a certain priest came down that road. And when he saw him, he passed by on the other side. Likewise a Levite, when he arrived at the place, came and looked, and passed by on the other side. But a certain Samaritan, as he journeyed, came where he was. And when he saw him, he had compassion. So he went to him and bandaged his wounds, pouring on oil and wine;

and he set him on his own animal, brought him to an inn, and took care of him. On the next day, when he departed, he took out two denarii, gave them to the innkeeper, and said to him, "Take care of him; and whatever more you spend, when I come again, I will repay you." So which of these three do you think was neighbor to him who fell among the thieves?

And he said, "He who showed mercy on him."

Then Jesus said to him, "Go and do likewise."

Luke 10:30–37

Did you see it? Jesus says there was a "certain man," a "certain priest," and a "certain Samaritan." The word *certain* to me strongly implies that Jesus is talking about actual people, not merely make-believe characters. I am aware that many theologians might take issue with me here, and I confess most of those guys are so intelligent that they have forgotten more than I'll ever know about Scripture. But I find it interesting that most translations include the word *certain*. So it may be my spiritual imagination getting the best of me here, but even if it is, assuming that Jesus is telling a real story about real people has helped the story become more alive to me. I believe God's Word is alive!

One of my dear friends and accountability partners is Mark Hall, front man for the contemporary Christian music group Casting Crowns. He asked me to preach a short, seventeen-second byte for the song "The Word is Alive" on their *Altar and the Door* CD. It's a great song highlighting the life-giving power of God's Word. I was privileged to join them in this exclamation by saying, "The Bible was inscribed over a period of two thousand years; in times of war and in days of peace; by kings, physicians, tax collectors, farmers, fishermen, singers, and shepherds. The marvel is that a library so perfectly cohesive could have been produced by such a diverse crowd over a period of time, which staggers the imagination. Jesus is its grand subject, our good is its design, and the glory of God is its end."

Let me encourage you to place your ear like a stethoscope on the chest of the story Jesus is telling. In so doing, we will hear the heartbeat of the living Word of God together.

It's important to note that Jesus's story comes as a reply to a question. A lawyer who was hired by religious leaders to snare Jesus in his words asked, "Who is my neighbor?" I don't think he really wanted to know who his neighbor was; it was more of a diversion. Kind of like when I tell my youngest son to put his toys away before bedtime and he says, "How do I pick them up?" You can imagine the stare-down I bust on my son when this happens. I know he knows how to pick them up. He just wants to expand the time between my command and the moment he actually obeys me.

> *Place your ear like a stethoscope on the chest of the story Jesus is telling. In so doing, we will hear the heartbeat of the living Word of God together.*

Here's where I need to throw a little caution out to you. My personal experience and seventeen years of ministry suggests we are often guilty of this same kind of spiritual standoff. Be careful not to snub this admonition. If we are honest about it, we would confess that we have suffered through this deadlock on more than one occasion. We've just never done it right in the face of God—but this lawyer does.

In my mind's eye, I see Jesus's neck swiftly turn as he makes eye contact with his inquisitor. Can you imagine the emotional weight pressing on your conscience as the all-knowing eyes of Divinity drill deep through your pupils? But just like my son does, the lawyer plays dumb: "Gee, what's a neighbor?"

Agitated, Jesus shifts his gaze and begins to scan the large crowd of people who have gathered to see this showdown between the Lord and the lawyer. Like Jesus's stare, it's blistering hot outside. The crowd emanates the sweaty and smelly cologne of humanity. Restless from the heat, the religious elite, along with peasants, soldiers, and shepherds, begin to murmur among themselves. But complaints about discomfort will have to wait because the only thing this crowd wants to hear is the response that's about to roll off the lips of the one who has the power to subdue demons.

As the temperature begins to rise, so does the noise of the crowd—rivaling the decibels of an NFL stadium on opening game day. Those standing closest to Jesus have already tried to hush the crowd, but they are not having any luck at quieting down the others no matter how fast and frantically they wave their hands. Then suddenly, a strange reversal of audio physics takes place. A soft, mild voice overpowers the boisterous clamor and hijacks every ear.

"A certain man . . . ," Jesus begins his answer. As he does, his eyes are fixed on a man who looks like he could use a little attention from a doctor. Blood is seeping through a bandage on the wounded man's forehead. His left arm is supported with a sling, making it difficult to manage the crutches he now has to use because of a broken leg. His eyes are black and sunken, filled with a hurt deeper than any physical wound can cause. The wrinkles in his dark, tanned face proudly declare that he's been around a while. Like the damaged hull of a battleship that has returned home from war, his scarred and aged features declare he was close to death and hobbled away from it.

". . . went down from Jerusalem to Jericho," Jesus continues.

At the sound of those words, the hurting man's mind indentifies with a trip he recently took on that same road. He jumps as pain shoots through his leg, which causes him to lose his balance and drop a crutch. Thankfully, the trembling man is held up by the wall of people leaning in to hear Jesus as he continues the story.

"And he fell among thieves, who stripped him of his clothing, wounded him, and departed, leaving him half dead." Jesus's eyes are fixed on the hurting man, for he is the man Jesus is speaking about.

Uncomfortable with Jesus's stare, the man grumbles under his breath, "I'm certain alright—certain that any half-brained son of a carpenter could look at me and see an obvious altercation with trouble has occurred." At that, he quickly dismisses any prophetic powers his aching heart had hoped might be in this professed Messiah. Fumbling for his fallen crutch, he bends over and with outstretched fingers focuses on reaching his wooden walking assistant, all the while concentrating on keeping his balance. Jesus says one more sentence.

"Now by chance a certain priest came down that road."

At those words, the man collapses—internally. His soul is shaken to its core. *How could Jesus know? No one else was on that road*, the bandaged man thinks to himself. *I cried out for hours and there was no one, until I saw that pathetic priest!* The thought of what happened that day summons feelings of shock, hate, anger, and sorrow. The emotions swell like a flooding tide within his beaten body and bruised heart, threatening to delay his recovery. *If I ever see that priest again, I'm going to give him a piece of my mind!* he huffs. He is oblivious to the fact that the priest is significantly closer than he could imagine. And from the look on Jesus's face, he is not the only one wanting to give the pathetic priest some mind pie. Jesus is about to get all up in somebody's religious Kool-Aid.

D E L V E

What was your response to the idea that the Good Samaritan story was an actual event?

_____

_____

_____

Take a moment and write out your personal definition of a good neighbor.

_____

_____

_____

Today during lunch, ask a few of your friends to give you their definition of a good neighbor. Reflect a moment on their similarities and differences and record them here.

_____

_____

_____

What one thought caught your attention the most in this chapter? Why?

_____

_____

_____

Lord Jesus, I know you told this story over two thousand years ago, but help me to lean into your words as if you were speaking them for the first time. I do believe that your Word is alive, and I ask you to make it come alive in my heart as I take this unique journey into the Good Samaritan story. Amen.

3

Feeling Their Pain

That we may be able to comfort those who are in any trouble, with the comfort with which we ourselves are comforted by God.

2 Corinthians 1:4

The gash beneath the seeping bandage begins to throb. The victim flinches in agony as he presses his fingers on the wound to make sure the dressing is secure. But worse than the pain on his head, is the pain within it. Jesus's words have triggered his memory. Cringing with his eyes shut, scenes from the attack flash across the monitor of his mind. Blurry and partial images of barbaric men summon his fears. They were the kind of men he would never do business with, but with kicks, punches, and blows they left their calling card all over his body. They also left with everything he owned— money, clothes, and half his life.

It had started out as a great day. He was in a good mood. The sun was bright and the sky a breathtaking blue. He was energized to travel because there was business to conduct and friends to enjoy in Jericho. But in a split second it all changed. In an instant, everything in his life shifted from tranquility to terror. One moment his eyes were taking in the sky, the next moment they were taking a punch. One moment he was soaking in the warmth of the sun, the next he was soaked in a pool of blood. This life change was brought to him courtesy of the thieves.

I've heard many people say, "That's what you get when you walk the streets in that part of town." "You can expect that kind of trouble when you stroll through a neighborhood like that." "He should have never been there in the first place!" The only problem with those statements is that we all live in a bad neighborhood. It's called *earth*, and it's under a curse. When Adam and Eve fell in the Garden, they sowed a bad seed, and now we are stuck with the fruit.

Sadly, the kind of calamity experienced by the traveler is a big part of the human experience. As a result, we can be full of life one moment and left half dead the next. It's hard to handle this kind of stark reality. Sometimes I have to laugh in order to keep myself from crying uncontrollably.

We all live in a bad neighborhood. It's called earth, and it's under a curse.

In high school I had a friend named Andy. Andy was a very interesting guy. He and I had nothing in common. First of all, I've always looked like an oversized elf and Andy was a mixture of young Elvis, Brad Pitt, and Zac Efron. He was what the ladies call a hottie. Girls would look at him and scream, "Oh Andy, you microwave my popcorn!" It was ridiculous. But what was more interesting about Andy is that he was plumb dumb. He had the IQ of a houseplant. A few dots missing off the dice. A little too much chlorine in the gene pool. A cute toy but the pull string was broken. Get the picture? So in order to get by, he would just be quiet. He didn't talk much, and when he did, it was always trouble.

One evening Andy and I came upon a traffic accident. A man on a motorcycle had been hit by a Mack truck. We jumped out to help. He was lying in the middle of the intersection all twisted up—an arm where there should be a foot, a foot where there should be an eye, and a nose where there should be a bottom. He looked like a human pretzel. A doctor and nurse, who had gotten out of their cars to help, tried to assist him, and he started cursing them out. I'm talking drunken sailor stuff. He screamed, yelled profanities, and really let us have it. All of us backed off as the man lay there yelling at us.

Well, do you remember Andy? Pull-string-broke Andy. He speaks—not good. Andy looked at the contorted motorcycle man and said, "Dude, you don't have to get all bent out of shape about it!" Oh, my word! I lost it. We all started laughing. Even the cussing sailor took a break from his foulness to cough out a couple of chuckles.

Knowing the man survived with just a few bruises makes it easier to laugh at that story. But what's not a laughing matter is what's happening to a countless number of people in neighborhoods, workplaces, schools, and families across our country. It has to do with the pursuit of happiness. I have never met a person who does not want to be happy. And in their quests, I've seen them drive down the highway of happiness on the motorcycle of life only to be broadsided by the Mack truck of the devil. Jesus said in John 10:10 that the devil, like the thieves in our story, is a thief who comes "to steal, and to kill, and to destroy." Satan lives to ambush humanity, and as a result there are millions of hurting people lying in the middle of the intersection of life, writhing in pain, drowning in a pool of their own emotional, mental, and spiritual blood—all bent out of shape. Victims of the ultimate relentless thug, they lie hemorrhaging with hurting hearts.

I know they do. Remember where I grew up? The streets in my neighborhood are stained with the red, life-giving fluid that flowed from the wounds of my soul. I identify with hurting hearts. I bet you do too. But have you talked with any of them lately? I've had numerous conversations with them in which we pulled up our emotional sleeves and exchanged stories about our scars. I wish I could forget the scars or even pretend they aren't there. So do the people with hurting hearts. But I'm learning that if you subject yourself to a bit of humble transparency, God will use your pain as a megaphone to cry out for those who can't anymore because their vocal cords are shredded from years of wailing.

If you subject yourself to a bit of humble transparency, God will use your pain as a megaphone to cry out for those who can't anymore.

My adversity started at birth. What I know about my biological mother comes from whispered conversations between adults I overheard as a child. Some said she was a prostitute. Others said she was worse than that because she would give herself away. As a result of her lifestyle, I was conceived. At birth I was placed in foster care, and my mother was placed in a mental institution for her own good. But my foster care experience was anything but good.

The first three years of my life I suffered unimaginable abuse at the hands of sick, twisted, perverted predators. I was just a baby and a little kid back then, so my mind remembers little, but my heart can't forget what happened to me. Through the same hushed conversations about my biological mother, I overheard fragments of heart-wrenching details of the maltreatment I endured. My so-called guardians regularly rolled me down flights of stairs. Evidently they thought it was a humorous sport to watch a tiny baby tumble into unconsciousness. They "disciplined" me by burning my arms with cigarettes. My behavior as a child strongly indicated that I suffered sexual molestation. My caregivers were more like thieves—pawns in Satan's hands carrying out his plan to steal my soul, kill my spirit, and destroy my heart. Experts say those early years are the most formative ones of a child's life. At three years of age I was already half dead.

When I was three, Bob and Dottie Nolan adopted me. I am grateful for my adoptive parents. They chose me, and for that I am eternally indebted. They adopted me for two hundred dollars, so I'm sort of a Wal-Mart special.

The good times outweighed the bad times in my family. But the bad times for me were really bad, and Satan used those moments to continue his assault for my soul. In the early years, we were very poor. I remember getting in fights at school when the other students made fun of my tattered hand-me-down clothes that were purchased from a local thrift store.

Our poverty wore heavy on my dad, and alcohol helped him cope. When he got drunk he became violent, and his anger would explode on me. I can recall the smell of whiskey on my dad's breath as he beat me and screamed in my face, "Is this all two hundred dollars got me? I wish I'd never bought you!" Those words crushed me. If you have ever sought the favor of someone you highly esteemed but got the opposite—total and complete rejection—you know it has a way of tearing your heart apart, little piece by little piece. My dad died of cancer when I was fifteen years old, and I never got to hear him say he loved me or was proud of me. His death meant I never got the chance to stitch up that part of my torn heart.

My father's rejection was a catalyst that propelled me to live a self-sabotaging lifestyle of massive alcohol and narcotics abuse. I had already been drinking and smoking pot from the early age of thirteen. But as the emotional anguish grew, so did my need for stronger drugs like cocaine, acid, and any other sedative that did not require a needle. I don't like needles. I had enough pain in my life, so I avoided anything that threatened to pierce any sensitive nerve. My goal was complete numbness.

Satan was bringing me down, and my descent reached its lowest as I began to wrestle with suicide. I was convinced that I wasn't even worth two hundred dollars. When you think you are worthless, it makes life worthless, and suicide can become an attractive option. Those were dark days in my life.

I can remember placing my dad's gun in my mouth. My entire body felt feverishly hot compared to the cold steel barrel of the .38 revolver. Sweat trickled from my forehead as I unsuccessfully strained for the courage to pull the trigger. On another occasion I recall the haunting feeling of a starchy rope around my neck as I wept and wished for someone to push me through my cowardliness and over the edge of the stairs in our house. No one came, and I couldn't jump. Those dark moments are seared indelibly in my memory. Even now I'm reminded of the taste of my tears that were shed in a mental ward in South Carolina where I was under a suicide watch because of a stupid stunt I attempted with some pills. I am vividly aware of the sorrow that torments those who are bent out of shape.

It's possible to be out of touch with the times, but because of my past, I don't think I will ever be out of touch with those who hurt. I don't want you to be out of touch with them either.

D E L V E

In what ways have you personally experienced the reality that earth is a bad neighborhood and is under a sin curse?

_____

_____

_____

Do you know anyone who is currently experiencing the "bent out of shape" factor in his or her life?

_____

_____

_____

What are some ways you have seen the devil steal, kill, and destroy lives?

_____

_____

_____

Pain that we experience can often be used to help others through their moment of crisis. In what way do you think God could use you in someone else's life?

_____

_____

_____

Jesus, I pause in this moment and ask you to help me do something. In my own power I will fail, but with your help I know it's possible. Enable me to take the painful moments of my life and use them to relieve some of the hurt others are enduring. If it brings you glory and advances your kingdom, it will be worth it all. Amen.

4

Called Out

The eyes of the LORD are in every place, keeping watch on the evil and the good.

Proverbs 15:3

Although I can identify with hurting hearts, I don't claim to be an expert on how to care for hurting people. But there is one thing I do know about them. My goal is to have this singular piece of understanding come alive in your heart. Let me give it to you. Here it comes; get ready to receive it. Are you leaning in? Okay, listen: *Hurting people need to see God.* I will say it again: *Hurting people need to see God.*

I know you were looking for something a bit more intellectually profound, but my personal experience tells me that just one glimpse of who God really is alters everything for the hopeless. And herein lies the great breakdown. Those who need to see the grace and mercy and compassion of God are instead seeing something entirely different in the lives of Christians. The wounded man in Jesus's story can testify to the pain that this rupture of representation can bring to a soul.

Allow your mind to travel back to the moment when Jesus is telling his story. The multitude of listeners is now silent, subdued by the graphic nature of the narrative. Their imaginations run wild wondering what will happen to the

> *Hurting people need to see God.*

casualty of crime who was left gasping for what might be his last breath. If anyone ever needed to see and encounter God, it was him.

> The people can almost see the dust that began to swirl into tiny funnels that licked across the dry, hot road, as the man lay near death. Volume high, Jesus's voice carries from the front to the back of the crowd, "A certain priest came down that road. . . ."
>
> The people begin to nod their shrouded heads toward each other—a gesture of anticipated hope for the troubled man. They can practically see him squinting through his swollen eyes. At first it was difficult for him to make out the blurry image of the figure walking toward him. But as the individual came into focus, it was apparent from the robe he wore that he was a priest.
>
> *He is going to be okay*, the people in the crowd think to themselves, *because a priest is coming*. They smile with approval. They are tracking with Jesus and know where this thing is going, and it has to be good with one of God's servants marching onto the scene. Our agonizing friend is about to have an encounter with someone who can connect him with the God who can heal.
>
> But the next sentence sends their eyebrows up and their mouths flying wide open. With his voice now the tone of a parent catching a child misbehaving, Jesus says, "And when he saw him, he passed by on the other side." The air

is instantly filled with a roar of disapproval from the crowd. They are aghast at such heartless conduct.

In the midst of the clamoring mass of humanity, a particular religious leader in the crowd seems very nervous. He isn't just any old priest; he is *the* priest.

Did you notice that the word I asked you to keep on your radar earlier comes out of Jesus's mouth again? It is the word *certain*. Remember, I believe this is not just a tale Jesus is telling. It is an actual event.

And that *certain priest* Jesus refers to is now ducking and weaving his way toward the edge of the crowd. His eyes are fixed on a tree in the near distance—a large tree he can hide behind or perhaps climb to safety if the swarming pack of disgruntled citizens discover who he is.

Then Jesus shifts his position and stands between the priest and the tree. The priest clutches his robe tightly around his body, but it fails to relieve the naked feeling engulfing him under the sovereign stare of Jesus. There will be no hiding place to conceal what he has done. The priest's heart pounds as it fights to resist the weight of guilt that is threatening to crush his religious pride. He is totally busted!

As Jesus stares down the priest, he begins to turn his face slowly toward the other side of the gathering. Then his eyes quickly shift and dial in on another person in the crowd. Jesus loudly declares, "Likewise a Levite, when he arrived at the place, came and looked and passed by on the other side."

You're way ahead of me here, aren't you? Yeah, you guessed it; the Levite is in the crowd as well. He, like the priest, is among the other listeners taking in the story.

KNOWING JESUS

As Jesus speaks, the Levite's stomach begins to knot up. There, among a couple hundred people he does not know, it is as if he is watching a video of a very shameful moment in his life taken by a hidden camera. The Levite remembers walking past the bloody mess on that road to Jericho, and now he is walking backwards, lips whistling and eyes to the sky, hoping to avoid detection.

Have you ever been busted like that before? Tammy and I have a hilarious video of our children when they got busted. Christy was four and Wil was two at the time. The video begins in the kitchen, focused on an empty countertop. Tammy says, "Where are my doughnuts? They are not here on the counter where I left them." The camera pans out, and you can see the adjoining dining area. You hear laughter, but no one is at the table. It's coming from under the table! The camera angles down and you see Christy and Wil with a box of doughnuts. Their mouths are full and their faces are covered with white powdered sugar. Christy clutches her savory plunder and races out of the room and clear of the camera. Wil does something that to this day we still tease him about. He keeps chewing the tasty cream-filled delight and shuts his eyes. Isn't that cute? Shutting his eyes was his way of hiding. His logic was, if he couldn't see you, you couldn't see him. Is that a riot or what? It's still the most requested family video in the house.

That's exactly the place where the priest and the Levite found themselves—only not so childlike and cute. They were totally busted. When confronted by Jesus, they probably shut their eyes hoping the moment would pass and they could return to their happy places. If you are ever called out by Jesus over something you did, I caution you to avoid that same response. You need to keep your eyes wide open as we identify elements of the breakdown that often occurs in our lives and causes hurting people to say, "Christianity sucks."

Without question, these two men were hurtful. I call them hurtful because of a personal conviction that I hold to. It goes like this: *Not to help is to hurt!* Let me write that again, and this time, you read it out loud: *Not to help is to hurt!*

Do you agree with that statement? Yeah, I thought you would. And that's why I call the priest and Levite *hurtful*. Some will say I am unfair to the priest and Levite because it was the thieves who left the man half dead. It's obvious that the robbers were the cause of the pain; however, the priest and Levite inflicted pain of their own.

How so? Think about it. When do you think the beaten man hurt the most? Was it before or after the religious men walked by? I emphatically believe it was after. Have you ever been hurting deeply and then come across a friend or family member whom you thought would lift you up because that's what they are supposed to do? But when you ran to them, did they seem oblivious to your hurt and simply hurry off to something that must have been more important? Having been there, I can tell you it leaves you hurting more than you were before.

Take a little *CSI* visit with me to the scene of the crime. Picture the man struggling for air, coughing up blood. Jesus says he was "half dead," meaning death was lurking at his door. As he lies there with eyes full of dirt, tears, and blood, the priest comes by. The man's heartbeat is faint, but upon seeing the priest he is inspired not to give up. I can hear him talking to himself, *You are going to make it. Help is here.* Crippled from the attack, he struggles but manages to lift up his hand and his voice to thank the priest for his help. But instead, in shock and disbelief he cries out, "Where are you going?" as the priest walks away.

If that were you, how would you feel in that moment? Refreshed? Invigorated? Oh no, it would feel like someone took a big syringe and extracted what remaining life may be struggling to survive in your chest cavity. And this happens to him twice! The wounds inflicted by the thieves were deepened by the neglect of the hurtful.

The priest and the Levite were representatives of God on earth. Remembering what they did to the hurting man, answer this question: Is that what God looks like? The answer is *no*. That's not the God we know. We read in Scripture that God is love. He sets captives free. He heals the brokenhearted and binds up their wounds. But is that the God the priest and the Levite showed?

An even more important question emerges from this story. Is this the God *we* show? Our flesh and this sin-cursed earth and all its pleasures lure us into being a part of the maddening breakdown between the God we know and the God we show. This misrepresentation of God is something I call *practical heresy*. We are going to do surgery on that term and on our hearts in the next chapter.

Jesus is calling you out. Don't shut your eyes. Open your heart, turn the page, and for the sake of the hurting, let the transformation continue.

D E L V E

In what ways would it be helpful for hurting people to see God?

_____

_____

_____

Write out your personal definition of what it means to be hurtful.

_____

_____

_____

If it is the case that *not to help is to hurt*, then write out a few ways you have seen this to be true in your life or the lives of others.

_____

_____

_____

What do you think needs to be reordered in your life to ensure that you are not guilty of being like the priest and Levite?

_____

_____

_____

God, I feel you calling me out. Pry my eyes open so that I don't shut them in an attempt to hide from my own faults. Help me to change for the sake of others who need your healing touch. Amen.

5

God's Skin

Awake to righteousness, and do not sin; for some do not have
the knowledge of God.

1 Corinthians 15:34

Continue this journey with me.

> As Jesus calls the priest and Levite out, they start moving
> away. One heads for a tree, the other goes racing anywhere
> to get away from the stare of Jesus. Scurrying to their
> prospective hideouts, the priest and Levite inadvertently
> run into each other. "Excuse me's" are expressed as they
> continue to move toward their evacuation routes. But then
> they run into someone they had run into before. Standing
> before them is the wounded man who was ambushed by
> thieves. Jesus sees it happen, and his smile indicates that he,
> like a master puppeteer, caused the collision. The hurtful are
> reunited with the hurting.
>
> The priest and Levite muse that the wounded man looks
> a bit taller standing up. The bandages confirm he is badly

hurt—more so than they would have imagined. At the sight of his injuries, their fear of being caught in wrongdoing is swallowed up by the gnawing realization of the wrong done.

When they first saw the man lying on the road, they were very careful not to make eye contact with him. Kind of like the way we avoid looking into the eyes of those who stand on street corners with "Will work for food" signs. Sure we look at them, but when they turn toward us, we snap our heads around and stare into nothingness as if it always had our attention.

Now eye-to-eye, they can feel his soul screaming louder than his voice ever did on the road. With eyes deep purple from the beating and deeper still with concern for others who may get attacked on that same road, the wounded man's soul quietly and compassionately begs them to change. His tears cry out, *Please don't ever do that to someone again!*

It's with that same spirit that I write these words. I'm not here to indict anyone; I just want to speak out for those who are hurting and beg you to do some serious inventory and make a life change that could change their lives.

In the first chapter I mentioned I was much like the outsiders. I did not grow up in the church. I shared certain beliefs and ideas about Christians that were very negative. Some of those faded once I was converted, but there are several that have proven shamefully true. The issue I referred to in the last chapter, *practical heresy*, is one of those shamefully true things. It is the single most destructive activity in the lives of those who claim to know God, and it causes distaste in the hearts of those who don't.

That's a big statement, huh? Sure it is, but I know it's true because I hang out with thousands of people all across America who are not Christians, and I am always asking them what is so bad about Christianity. This issue of practical heresy rises to the top of their accusations against us. I have to say I agree with them because I experienced it from the church as a child, and it extracted life out of my heart—a heart, if you remember, that was already half dead.

If they are accusing the vast majority of Christians of being practical heretics, then it's important to understand what the term means. A *heretic* is someone who teaches something about God that is theologically incorrect. Heresy usually shows up in our beliefs. For instance, if someone believes and teaches others that God is not holy, that person is called a heretic because Scripture clearly shows that God is without sin and is totally set apart from all other entities. But when we refer to *practical heresy*, we are referring not to beliefs but to behavior, not to doctrine but to deeds.

Practical heresy is the single most destructive activity in the lives of those who claim to know God, and it causes distaste in the hearts of those who don't.

The priest and Levite knew doctrine. They were required by tradition and law to memorize mass amounts of information about the books of the Law and about God. If you had a major question about a complicated theological issue, they could answer your questions correctly. And the idea that God would walk by those who have hurting hearts, well, that would never come out of their lips. But that's exactly the message they preached with their lives when they walked past the wounded man.

The priest and Levite are classic examples of the breakdown between the God that we know and the God that we show. This is the sad commentary of most Christians today. They give great detail to accuracy when filling in the blanks of their Bible study or sermon notes. But they often fail terribly when it comes to accurately filling in the blanks that outsiders have in their hearts about God.

When I was thirteen years old, I had an experience with some Christians that hurt me deeply and skewed my impression of God. Because of all the poverty, abuse, and drugs, my life was in shambles. To top it off, my dad was dying of cancer, and I was wrestling with how I felt about it. I was sad for my mom because she was losing her husband but happy for me because I would be free from his outbursts. Yet I was holding onto a dream that one day my adoptive father would tell me he loved me. I was sick in all kinds of ways, so when some people from a church's bus ministry knocked on my door and said they wanted me to go to church, I agreed to give it a try. Sadly, I had many hurtful experiences with the Christians who went to that church. I invite you to join me through one of those moments that constantly replays on the DVD of my memory.

Bam!

Without warning, pain raced through my brain and told me I was experiencing blunt trauma to my mouth. In a nervous reaction, my fingers raced to the point of impact and felt around to assess the damage. The sight of blood was unsettling, but it explained what that taste was in my mouth. I was bleeding because someone punched me in my face. My eyes went into radar mode to track down the assailant. Was it a thug? Had I unknowingly crossed his turf? Was it a thief who was after whatever loose change I had in my pocket? Who was attacking me?

It only took a second to shake out the cobwebs. Once focused, my eyes caught the attacker. It was the pastor's son! Sound shocking? Maybe not if you know a mean pastor's kid. But let me put this story into context.

This punch took place on a church bus. The God they followed mandated that they reach out to me and convert me. So through a bus ministry these Christians came into my impoverished neighborhood to pick me up for services. We had already gone to the service and were on our way home when the leader of the bus route began prayer time. I was not a praying person. I was an outsider and an ADD outsider at that. During prayers I was normally freaking out about a bug on the window or a dog outside in someone's front yard. So while they were praying, I was doing what outsiders do, and the pastor's son tried to ram his fist down my throat for not praying. Great evangelistic strategy! Seriously, I was stunned. The first thing I wanted to do was take the number-two pencil the nerd had in his pocket and shove it though his temple. Violent, I know, but I was a ghetto kid and violence was often the only way I knew to survive.

This boy was a Christian, and I had just been told in the service that Christians are Jesus with skin. I was terrible at math, but my mind did some quick addition, and the sum said that I just got punched in the mouth by God because he hates outsiders who don't pray. That was the day I began thinking Jesus was much like my adoptive father—angry, disappointed in me, and violent. This is a mindset I carried with me through many years of my life.

> *Non-Christians have heard us say that we are his body; therefore, they think that the way we treat them is the way God feels about them.*

I have never forgotten that moment on the bus. It reminds me to be careful how I treat outsiders. It is true we are Jesus with skin. Non-Christians have heard us say that we are his body; therefore, they think that the way we treat them is the way God feels about them. That was my experience as a teenager, and it is an insight Christians need to be mindful of.

You may be high-fiving yourself because you've never punched anyone in the mouth on a church bus. Kudos to you for that! At least you're not like the jerk who gave me a knuckle sandwich. But we are all guilty of punching outsiders.

For instance, over the last seventeen years of being an insider in the church, I have seen Christians hold their noses and whisper hurtful words to their friends as a dirty, hungover, homeless person squeezed into their pew. I've witnessed

Christians cast judgmental glances at a visitor in the church parking lot who was smoking a cigarette. I've watched church members jab with their words by telling a divorcée that she is a whore. I've observed zealous believers stand outside an abortion clinic and scream into the face of a pregnant teenager that she is a murderer. And I've thrown my share of jabs by judging, being preachy, and being too busy to care for others because I was preoccupied with my to-do list for the day.

What I have experienced tells me that we are prone to be worse than the priest and Levite ever were. At least they kept their mouths shut and moved on. But just like they did, we often misrepresent God to the hurting people who are crippled by sin and in need of rescue. Those who need to see the grace, mercy, and compassion of God instead too often see, by our lives, something entirely different.

If you recall the statistics in the beginning of this book, you know that a high percentage of people in our culture have suffered from practical heresy. I think you will agree that something desperately needs to change. They need to see God for who he really is—and a picture of what that looks like is personified in Jesus's story by the next character: the "certain Samaritan."

D E L V E

Describe a moment when you were eye-to-eye with the poor, needy, or homeless. How did they make you feel? What thoughts went through your mind about them?

_____

_____

_____

Don't go back through the chapter, but from memory try to draft a few sentences that describe what *practical heresy* is. After you have done this, go back through the chapter and compare your sentences with what I wrote. What elements were missing and what elements did you dial in on?

_____

_____

_____

Explain a few ways you think practical heresy is sending a negative message about Jesus.

_____

_____

_____

God, I confess that I am prone to misrepresent you to others. I so desire that those moments become less frequent, and I commit that day by day I will try to be mindful of my conduct toward outsiders. This I do as an act of worship to you, knowing that you care deeply for those who don't know you yet. Amen.

6

Hurt Healer

Observe these things without prejudice, doing nothing with partiality.

1 Timothy 5:21

Jesus's smile widens as he watches the priest and Levite race away. The hurting man's face reflects a tinge of closure. He hasn't felt good for months since the attack, and now he feels triumphant—like a hero who has stopped a big bully from picking on a small child. He displayed his scars, and they spoke loudly and passionately against their injustice, which was something he had desired to do ever since those men walked past him on that dreadful road.

Jesus studies the look of satisfaction on the hurting man's face, and it stirs him to continue driving home the point he is making to the lawyer. As he begins to speak again, birds dart a little too close over the heads of the large, boisterous crowd, but no one seems to notice them. Nor do they notice that the very people Jesus is talking about are right under their noses. The only thing that is clear to them is the great disregard they have in their hearts for anyone who claims to be a God follower yet shuts his or her eyes and ears to the cry of the hurting. It wouldn't be a stretch to say that the people who are outsiders in our world of influence feel the same way.

Someone in the crowd shouts, "Find the scoundrels and beat them!" Then the multitudes join in with shouts of "Yeah!" "Do it now!" "Let's turn them over to the thieves!" Shouts are being hurled and the faces in the throng are contorted in disapproval.

Then with just four words spoken very softly, Jesus silences the crowd. The hush saturates the mob because one of the four words Jesus uses is far more repulsive to this crowd than the phrase "Christianity sucks" is to most church people.

Jesus's eyes are bright with anticipation as he smiles and says calmly, "But a certain Samaritan. . . ."

At the sound of these words, the mob's disapproval suddenly transfers from the hurtful heretics to Jesus. If looks could kill, this moment would be Jesus's crucifixion. The hatred of the shepherds, religious leaders, fishermen, and farmers toward the priest and Levite is mild compared to the seething venom that is now dripping from the corners of their frowns. The cries of violence have escalated now into a vocal vortex of rage—and it is all aimed at Jesus!

What has caused this sudden shift in animosity? It's because Jesus said a nine-letter word that is as vile to their ears as some four-letter words are to ours. What word could possibly cause such intense upheaval and emotional distress? It is the word *Samaritan*.

To understand why this word had such crowd-silencing, anger-inciting power, you need only an elementary understanding of what a Samaritan was. You see, a Samaritan was a blotch on the race of the Jews. They were half-breeds who were brought into existence through rape. As a weapon of war, the Romans raped the Jewish women to pollute their pure Jewish race. The babies born out of that twisted violence were called Samaritans. Life for a Samaritan was filled with prejudice, isolation, rejection, and unkindness—similar to the segregation that infected America in the 1950s and '60s. Samaritans were not allowed to eat, play, work, or interact on any level with Jews. They were required to live on the outskirts of Jewish towns and were never given a chance to improve their lives. And by the looks on the faces of those gathered around Jesus, a Samaritan would be the least likely person to ever be seen as a hero in a rescue drama. As I think about what might have been going on as Jesus was telling this story, I picture him getting a little concerned.

> As the word *Samaritan* rolls off his lips, Jesus takes a drink from a water jug. The faces in the crowd begin directing their cutting glances toward him as he swallows the cool water with a loud gulp and wipes the sweat off his brow. He's not nervous about what the crowd may do to him—not one bit. He's able to dodge people and mysteriously free himself from the hands of angry mobs. His anxiety is for the certain Samaritan.

The word *certain*, remember, clues us in to the idea that this outcast is real and is probably close by. I don't imagine he is among the throng. He is a Samaritan and is not welcome. But I think he is close enough for the angry mob to do him harm. And Jesus knows they would because this prideful crowd would never let a Samaritan win the Oscar in a story in which God's priest and Levite, no matter how unworthy, should be the ones getting the rave reviews.

Thousands of years ago the mob hated Jesus. Yet I find it interesting that over time this attention-getting *certain*

Samaritan has gained favor among those who have heard his story. This cannot be denied because he actually went from being called "a certain Samaritan" to being called "the Good Samaritan." If you read the story carefully, you will notice that Jesus never calls him a "good" Samaritan. He simply calls him a Samaritan. But as this story has been told millions of times over the course of thousands of years, this man went from being a plain old *certain* Samaritan to a *good* Samaritan. How did he get this name change? I think it's because people remember you for your testimony, not your title.

Martin Luther King Jr. said his dream was that one day black Americans would not be judged by the color of their skin but by the content of their character. That is exactly what happened here. After Jesus told this story, people began to tell their versions of it. As they did, they kept all the details the same except that they began to label the Samaritan according to the content of his character.

I like that we call him the Good Samaritan. But I don't think we have been giving him enough credit. You see, in the Nolan family we like to dial in on things. If one of my children does something good, we acknowledge it. I am big on this thing, people. Simply saying, "Thanks for the help," is not acceptable in the Nolan home. No sir. We dial in on what was actually done. So if someone helps with the dishes we say, "Thank you for your help; you are a great dishwasher." I don't just say, "You are a good boy." I want my son to know what I am grateful for, and I want his siblings to know exactly what was commendable.

Now let's apply that to the Samaritan. If we dial in on the Good Samaritan's conduct, I think it would be most appropriate to call him the Hurt Healer. You may be asking what a *hurt healer* is and why we should call the Good Samaritan one. In the next three chapters we are going to break down the Samaritan's DNA and in so doing, fully define the profile of a hurt healer. For starters, though, a *hurt healer* is the opposite of a *hurtful heretic*. Hurt healers are active and even proactive. They look for ways to help the down-and-outers. They have been hurt themselves; they know what it feels like to hurt deeply and want to be rescued. Hurt healers are different from religious jerks in that they don't *talk* about serving, they *walk* about serving.

I love to listen to preaching. I just can't get enough of it. I purchase CDs of great speakers, and I subscribe to tons of podcasts. I listen to them in my car or on my iPod while I'm running. And I take lots of notes—of course not when I'm driving! As a result of all this preaching intake, I have files and files of sermon notes. From time to time I get those notes out and read them over. You may do this as well, and if so, you know the great wellspring of refreshment you get from this practice. If you don't, I invite you to start the discipline of taking notes. I always glean something from them.

> **Hurt healers know what it feels like to hurt deeply and want to be rescued.**

As I was preparing for this book, I ran across a page of notes that I took from someone who was preaching about the Good Samaritan story. I don't have the name of the preacher (I didn't say I was a great note taker), but I did get his point. He said there are three types of people in the story—the takers, the fakers, and the difference maker. The thieves were the takers, the priest and Levite were the fakers, and the Samaritan was the difference maker. Each of these guys had a particular philosophy about life that governed his actions. The takers believed, *What's yours is mine and I am going to take it*. The fakers thought, *What's mine is mine and I am going to keep it*. The difference maker said, *What's mine is yours and I am going to give it*. That's the heartbeat of a hurt healer, and I am convinced that if more Christians caught that kind of heart, we would see a major shift in our nation's mindset about Jesus and Christianity.

Why do you think we have such a disregard for people when they hurt others but we seem to be able to justify our own hurtful conduct?

_____

_____

_____

Prejudices are not limited to the color of skin. Name a few that you have seen or experienced from the church.

_____

_____

_____

The Good Samaritan wins the Oscar in this emotional drama. The crowd disapproves, but God delights in it. How did you respond? Why?

_____

_____

_____

I gave the Good Samaritan a new name, Hurt Healer, in order to more appropriately dial in on his conduct. Try to articulate what went through your mind when you read about that.

_____

_____

_____

*God, keep my heart from the evil prejudices that
infect many churches. Set my heart aflame to be a
lover of all humanity. Grant me grace to emulate the
conduct of this Hurt Healer. Amen.*

7

Pausing for Compassion

Hold such men in esteem; because for the work of Christ he came close to death, not regarding his life, to supply what was lacking in your service toward me.

Philippians 2:29–30

Picking up his fallen crutch, the wounded man wipes off the dust, puts it under his arm, and begins to hobble a little closer to this apparent prophet named Jesus. At first he was skeptical about the claims of others that Jesus is truly sent from God. But not only can he still see the hurtful heretics pass him by, but now Jesus seems to be revealing that he knows even more about that day. The man has to hear more.

Competing with the noise of the crowd, Jesus raises his voice almost to a full scream and proclaims, "A certain Samaritan, as he journeyed, came where the man was. And when he saw him, he had compassion. So he went to him and bandaged his wounds, pouring on oil and wine. And he set him on his own animal, brought him to an inn, and took care of him. On the next day when he departed, he took out two denarii, gave them to the innkeeper, and said to him, 'Take care of him; and whatever more you spend, when I come again I will repay you.'"

As Jesus speaks, the volume of his voice becomes lower as the crowd begins to hush once again. They get really quiet. The crowd's prejudices are subdued by the action the Samaritan took to combat the very thing they were upset about in the first place—injustice. They are ashamed.

But shame is not Jesus's intent. He wants to inspire them. He wants their souls stirred so deeply that they rally together and forge a movement of hurt healers to meet the needs of their neighbors.

That's exactly my goal here with you. I want us to lean in and check out the conduct of this Hurt Healer and join the movement of God in touching lives for his glory.

If we are to be hurt healers, let's look at the DNA of the guy who was formerly known as the Good Samaritan and is currently called the Hurt Healer (well, in my world anyway). There are three things this guy did that I want us to focus on: he *paused* for compassion, he *proved* he cared, and he *paid* the cost. I don't usually do alliterated outlines, but those three thoughts jumped out at me in my study of this guy. Let's look at each one of these over the next several chapters and consider them for action steps that we might merge into our own lifestyle.

One of the reasons hurt healers make such a difference in someone's life is because they pause for compassion. I like to define *compassion* as simply "love in action." When hurt healers see a need, they put everything else on hold in order to engage the need. They exchange their to-do list for a must-do moment. The Samaritan was on a journey. He had something to do, people to see, and places to go. But when he saw a man on the road who had been ambushed by thieves and was half dead, everything else had to wait. Nothing was more important to him than making sure the half-dead guy was resuscitated. He put all other tasks on pause to show some love to a man who needed it. I like this guy; I like him a lot. The world would be a better place if there were more people like him. Maybe that's Jesus's point as well.

When hurt healers see a need, they put everything else on hold in order to engage the need.

Sometimes when I'm reading a story in the Bible, I imagine myself interviewing the people in the story. It sounds a little weird, I know. But it has been helpful for me in developing a heart connection with what otherwise is to me mere words on a page. Oh don't get me wrong; the Bible is God's authoritative Word. My imaginary interactions just help the Word come alive for me. God uses them to broaden my capacity to wrap my head and heart around the story.

I conducted an imaginary interview with the Hurt Healer. I wanted to find out what made him tick. What did he have going on in his mind that helped him hear the cry of the hurting heart?

> **Me:** Mr. Hurt Healer, thank you for taking the time to meet with me today. I have just a few questions for you and then I'll let you go.
>
> **Hurt Healer:** No problem, ask away. Oh, and by the way, I really dig the name change thing. Thanks for the thoughtfulness.
>
> **Me:** You're welcome. Just a little something we do in the Nolan home. First of all, why were you on your way to Jericho?
>
> **Hurt Healer:** I don't remember. I went there all the time. I was just going about my weekly routine.
>
> **Me:** Tell me in your words what was going through your mind when you saw the hurting person on the road.
>
> **Hurt Healer:** Well, to be honest, the first thing that came to my mind was, "I don't have time for this." I don't remember why I was headed to Jericho, but I do know I was in a hurry. I'm always in a hurry.

56

Me: Yeah, I know the feeling, and so will all of the people who read this interview. So what caused you to stop?

Hurt Healer: At first I thought he was dead. He looked awful, and there was a lot of blood. He wasn't moving. Then suddenly his body convulsed and shook violently, and he gasped for a breath. As I was riding by, I caught a glimpse of his eyes. He was crying. His tears were streaking through the blood and dirt on his face. But his tears were not just from the pain; he was incredibly sad. I know because I've been there. As a Samaritan, I've taken my share of kicks to the face and head. I would like to give blood at the blood drive, but I never have enough to spare. But worse than any of the kicks to the head were the jabs at my heart when someone would . . . when they would. . . .

Me: I understand it's tough to talk about. We can stop if you need to.

Hurt Healer: No, I'm okay. It's worth living it again if I know someone reading this book will be different because of my pain. It crushed me when someone made fun of my non-Jewish dad and insulted me by calling me a half-breed who would never amount to anything. I always wrestled with doing what my angry heart felt like doing: fighting back, kicking them until their minds were senseless, and cursing them so loudly that their ears would bleed. But my mother and my grandparents taught me to always do the right thing and force my heart to follow.

Me: Well, why was this guy someone you had a hard time helping? You didn't even know him did you?

Hurt Healer: He was hard to recognize at first. But once I started cleaning him off, I recognized him as the bully who used to beat me up almost every day and who rallied others to hate me as well. But I remembered what it felt like for me when I was lying there bleeding, crushed, and hurting. I can't do to others what they have done to me. I must do to others as I want done to me. If I picked and chose those I will love, I'd feel filthy. I must love everyone—even those who have hurt me.

Me: Wow! I'm blown away. I'm such a loser; I would never do that. I would have run over him with my donkey. I would have finished him off and excused it as an act of mercy. I am so unlike you. But there is something in me that wants to be like you in every way. Thanks for being an example. You have proven an old saying to be false. It says that "hurt people hurt people." Meaning if someone has been hurt, that person is sure to repeat that hurt to others. Having been hurt myself, I hated hearing that because I also know we become what we believe about ourselves. You have given hope to more than just that guy on the road that day. You are living proof that "hurt people help people."

See, wasn't that interview helpful to your heart? I know in the biblical account we don't have these details, and I am not trying to add to the Bible here. I just played out in this interview with the Hurt Healer what I have heard hundreds of times from present-day, real-life people that I've seen working with the homeless, serving in a soup line, and volunteering in disaster relief. I have met people who have been hurt deeply, and I have seen them serve the very ones who had caused them great distress. What a testimony to the capacity of the human heart to be authentically compassionate.

I always walk away from those people feeling really bad about my own life. I get ambushed with the shame of how short I fall. But then I remember that shame is not God's intent; his intent is inspiration. So I choose to rid myself of my insecurities and instead let their acts of love, grace, forgiveness, and compassion be a catalyst for change in my own sphere of influence.

D E L V E

Jesus uses the example of the Hurt Healer to inspire change, not to shame the crowd. Name a person who lived so extraordinarily that he or she inspired you to change. What was so special about that person?

_____

_____

_____

What virtues must be present in your heart for you to exchange your to-do list for a must-do moment?

_____

_____

_____

Try to recall a moment when you saw compassion fleshed out in someone's life. What emotions did you see displayed between the giver and receiver? How did it make you feel when you witnessed that moment?

_____

_____

_____

If you had a chance to interview Mr. Hurt Healer, what questions would you ask him?

_____

_____

_____

_Urgency has a way of preoccupying my mind and
heart. Lord, help me to pause this day and put love
into action with those who are hurting. I choose to
prove my faith in you by being ready to put aside my
to-do list for a must-do moment if and when it arises
during my day. Amen._

8

Proving We Care

By faith Enoch was taken away so that he did not see death, "and was not found, because God had taken him"; for before he was taken he had this testimony, that he pleased God.

Hebrews 11:5

After hearing Jesus give the details of the attack he had suffered, the victim has a whole new look on his face. He has lost his skepticism. His eyes twinkle and his lips slowly curve upward in a smile as he ponders how Jesus knows everything that happened that day.

Hearing the reenactment sparks flashes of emotion he has not felt in a long time. He has been trying so hard to bounce back that he has not taken the time to look back. Eyes still fixed in amazement on Jesus, his hand involuntarily presses into his cheek and his finger runs across the outline of a scar left behind by the thieves. As he holds his face in his hand, he tries desperately to remember what the Hurt Healer looks like. *One day I would love to run into him and say thanks*, he muses.

Murmurs of mixed emotions are spreading around the crowd, but there is nothing mixed about his feelings toward the Hurt Healer. He is beyond fond of him. *What if he is close by just like the priest and Levite were?* he wonders. His eyes dart across the faces in the crowd. But he doesn't even know what he looks like. Closing his eyes tightly, he tries to recall any of the features that would make him stand out in the crowd. Was he tall, short, skinny, husky, brown-haired, or bald?

Zap! A phantom pain races through the back of his head. They are occurring less frequently lately, but the pain is intense when it comes on. The back of his head is where he took the first blow from the thieves, and when he fell from the hit, he smashed his forehead on the road. That's when everything began spinning, followed by screaming intermingled with kicks and stabs.

He squints a bit harder trying to shake the memory of the attackers and summon any small shred of remembrance of the Hurt Healer. It's useless! He can't remember his features, but he will never forget his kindness. Life was ebbing slowly out of him that day, and he knew death was breathing down his neck and had come to wield its blow. Then suddenly death tucked tail and fled, unable to finish off its prey because the Hurt Healer stepped in and saved the day.

His smile widens as he remembers all the Samaritan did for him. At the thought of the bandages, the oil, and the wine, his lips press together and he rolls his tongue across them recalling the taste of the exhilarating liquid the Samaritan gently poured down his throat. Then he remembers seeing a flower as he was laid over the man's donkey. It was growing up through the hardened, rocky soil, suggesting that life must fight to survive the harsh elements on earth. He determined to hold on.

The smoothness of the flower petals bring to mind the completely relaxing feeling of snuggling into the cozy bed at the inn. Oh, and who could forget the food at the inn. It was the best he had ever eaten! Hot eggs for breakfast, bread and raisins for lunch, and the oven-roasted lamb for dinner was succulent. And what about the free room and board for a whole month? That's how long it had taken him to be able to get up and head on his way.

Tears begin rolling down his cheeks as he remembers going to the innkeeper to pay and hearing him say, "The fellow who brought you in has already taken care of your bill, and if you need to take food for your journey, he has taken care of that as well."

The man's weeping grabs the attention of people in the crowd. Jesus sees him as well, and even his eyes fill with tears. Divinity is moved deeply when his creation is comforted.

What this man was feeling is the point behind Jesus's story. He longs for humanity to care deeply for one another and help each other through the pain of this sin-cursed world.

The swarm of people taking in Jesus's words each would have said that they would care for a guy who is down and out. But the Hurt Healer went beyond simply saying he cared—he showed he cared. He didn't just go the second mile with his service either. He took it as far as it needed to go. Think about it. He stopped and put all other priorities on hold.

The Hurt Healer went beyond simply saying he cared—he showed he cared.

He rolled up his sleeves and got dirty by bandaging and tending the man's wounds. Then he went over the top with some crazy love by funding the man's recovery. He gave the innkeeper two denarii. Do you know how much money that was? It was two days' wages. How about that for some serious love? A lot of bad things may be said about a Samaritan, but one thing they can't say about this one is that he didn't care. This Hurt Healer proved he cared, and the result was a healed heart.

Once in Dallas, Texas, I saw a billboard wrap on a city bus. It was a black-and-white photo of an impoverished girl from Malawi in southeastern Africa. Her skin was hanging from her bones, and her eyes were bulging from her skull from malnourishment. It was a shocking photo. The caption beside it was equally penetrating: "It's enough to make you cry, but is it enough to make you help?" God used that billboard to arrest my heart that day. So much of the outsiders' criticism is on target because most Christians only gather together in their small groups and Sunday morning services and cry about the plights of the unfortunate. It's good to cry, but at some point we need to merge our crying with some caring. That's what hurt healers do. They don't just profess they care; they prove they care.

D E L V E

Take a moment and write out your personal definition of *caring*.

_____

_____

What was the prevailing thought that kept rising to the surface as you read about how the hurting man recalled the care he received from the Hurt Healer?

_____

_____

I said that Divinity is moved deeply when its creation is comforted through caring. Look back at the last month of your life. What emotions have you caused to swell up in the heart of God through your service to others?

_____

_____

_____

Looking at the last question, describe some ways that you would like to see your answer be an even better one in the future.

_____

_____

_____

Knowing that people feel deeply, let me be moved even deeper to care for them. O God, I repent of being so caught up in my own interests that I fail to be interested in others. Cultivate within me a caring heart for hurting hearts. Amen.

9

Paying the Cost

He who has pity on the poor lends to the Lord, and He will pay back what he has given.

Proverbs 19:17

In his story, Jesus said a guy gave away two denarii and then also told an innkeeper that he would pay whatever more the victim needed to get better. "You spend; I will repay." Those words were still echoing through the mind of the silenced crowd listening to Jesus. When someone does something with money that seems crazy, it always steals the spotlight.

I will be honest with you; this chapter will challenge you to your core. I'm guessing here, but I am thinking that many who are reading this will probably be tempted to stop reading right now, look at the table of contents, and move on to a chapter with a sweeter title that doesn't deal with money. As a fellow member of the "looking for the money tree" club, I understand. But what if there was a way to get the things you need by meeting the needs of others? Would you keep reading? Sure you would. Well, I think I have broken the code on this money thing here. So I invite you to keep reading.

Remember the interview I had with Mr. Hurt Healer? Well, let's go back and pick up where I left off.

Me: Dude, I know that Jesus said you gave away two days' wages, and he never lies. But it sounds so crazy that I gotta ask. Did you really?

Hurt Healer: Yes, I did. But I never intended for anyone except the innkeeper to know about it.

Me: Well, now everybody who reads the Bible or hears a sermon about your story knows. How does that make you feel?

Hurt Healer: A little weird; kind of like writing a love note to someone and getting caught by the teacher, who reads it out loud to the class. It was meant to be personal, but no biggie.

Me: Well, as it relates to the two denarii, according to the story you had the money on you, so I'm guessing you were going to do something else with it. Am I correct?

Hurt Healer: Yes, I was. Now that you ask, I recall that one of the reasons I was headed to Jericho was to purchase some new sandals. Being that we have no cars, I pretty much walk everywhere, and my sandals had a hole worn through the bottom. I was also going to purchase a knife to hunt with and use for protection. Most of the roads I travel can turn violent in a flash.

Me: I see you have a new pair of shoes on now, and that looks like a knife hanging from your belt. How did you get those items if you gave the money away?

Hurt Healer: Amazing, isn't it? I'm always taken aback by God's economics. When I was a child, my grandparents read words from Solomon's parchments to me. Money is one of the biggest issues in most people's lives. They live for it and die without it. One of Solomon's sayings went something like this: "A man who gets and keeps has nothing, but a man who scatters has more." My family taught me to be a giver. And to this day, God amazes me because I have never missed what I have given away. And it doesn't always happen, but many times, through the provision of God, I still end up getting the thing I was going to purchase with the money I gave away.

Me:	Earlier I told you I was so not like you when you were mending the wounds of those who hurt. I have been hurt a lot as well, and God is molding me to become more like you in that area. But in this area of giving, I'm tracking with you big time. Can I tell you about it?
Hurt Healer:	I would love to hear about it.
Me:	Okay, but remember, all of the glory goes to Jesus.

Before I met Jesus, I was stingy. My stinginess was so bad that I wouldn't just keep what I had, I would take what you had too! Last time I checked, I think that kind of person is called a thief. That's what I was, but after I met Jesus, he changed me and gave me a heart to give.

My journey into giving started when I became a Christian. Shortly after becoming a believer, I was living in a Volkswagen van. It had a two-tone, sky-blue top with a lime green body. It was so rusty. Huge chunks of missing metal were covered by bumper stickers. I remember one that I placed right in the front below the windshield. It said, "Know Jesus, know peace! No Jesus, no peace." We're talking a true old-school hippie van.

Times were tough for me in those days. I was struggling from job to job with no money in the bank and only five dollars to my name. I was very depressed about my financial situation, which led me to be angry with God. I remember thinking, "Wow, here I am not partying anymore, keeping myself away from the sinful things of this world, and God has abandoned me." Where was the abundant life I heard so many preachers talk about?

I remember one day when my stomach started to growl. I pulled into a deli, walked in, and purchased a three-dollar deal that included a dried-out chicken wing, a stale biscuit, and a flat Sprite. I drove away and parked the van near a bridge by St. Johns River in Jacksonville, Florida. I find it funny now to think that I was living in a van down by the river long before I was a motivational speaker. (That was for all of us Chris Farley fans.) My lunch tasted terrible, and the bitterness in my heart was even worse. I remember screaming out all kinds of mean things at God. Then in tears I said, "What am I supposed to do?"

And God spoke to me loudly and clearly: "Give!"

"Give what?" I asked.

"Everything in your pocket and all you can for the rest of your life."

Freaked out that I actually heard God speak to me, I went to church that Wednesday night. During the service they passed a big bronze plate around. I put in my last two dollars. And then God did a miracle. I'm talking a Red Sea–splitting miracle!

Before I left the church building that night, I had way more money in my pocket than I had put into the plate. And no, I didn't steal from the offering plate. There were people who did not even know me who came up and said, "Hey, God laid you on my heart. Please take this." And they put cash in my hand. Wow! One moment I was standing there broke, and the next I was holding over a hundred dollars in my hand! I didn't know at that point that the Bible says give and it shall be given unto you.

Hurt Healer: Your story is proof that God is great. I have always known this, and that's why I'm never fearful of giving.

Me: Me neither, but I want to make sure that I clarify something about this giving thing. I'm not saying God is some sort of cosmic vending machine, where you put something in and cha-ching, you get more out. No, not at all. God is not about cash, castles, and Cadillacs. But what I am saying is that God is crazy about blessing people who have chosen to not let money be their master but instead make it their servant by giving generously. God's Word encourages us by telling us that God is scanning the hearts of everybody in the world, on the hunt for anybody whose heart is out to bring him glory. That person will experience the mighty power of God on his or her behalf. And I am here to testify that he does what he says he will do.

I have been in this relationship with Jesus, tithing and giving for over twenty years, and he has stunned me with his sufficiency. I have scores of stories of how he has provided for me after asking me to give. Recently, God asked me to give big, and I was freaking out because I didn't think I could. I was trying to save thirty thousand dollars to adopt our little girl from China, Joy Fei Fei. One day God told me to give a thousand dollars to a couple to pay for their rent, utilities, and food for the month. I wrestled with it, but then I scraped up the money and gave it. Within the week, I got a check in the mail for $1,200.00 and a note that said, "God gave this to me, then he told me to give it to you."

I can testify that God blesses those who choose to bless others through giving. My life is invigorated by living above the economic paradigm of this world. In giving, we free ourselves from the trap of humanistic living and we get to experience our God supernaturally interacting with us.

> *God is crazy about blessing people who have chosen to not let money be their master but instead make it their servant by giving generously.*

The greatest giver I know is my pastor, Dr. Johnny Hunt. He is always saying, "You are never more like Jesus than when you are giving." I believe that. I believe that if we all decided to step it up and be hurt healers who pay the cost, those who are hurting would see a new, fresh, and clearer picture of what our Lord Jesus is really like.

D E L V E

Financial stewardship can evoke a wide range of reactions. Describe the thoughts and emotions you have after reading this chapter.

_____

_____

_____

How could your current life be different if you chose to live under God's economic paradigm?

_____

_____

_____

Think of some people in need. How would they feel today if you gave something to them that they need? Could it ignite their faith?

_____

_____

_____

What did you think about my testimony that I shared with the Hurt Healer? Write out something you have experienced as a result of being a giver.

_____

_____

_____

Lord Jesus, you came to give. I agree with Dr. Hunt's statement that I am never more like you than when I am giving. I don't want to paint a poor picture of you for outsiders to see. Change my heart and fuel my faith to give in such a way that it reflects your extravagant giving heart for the hurting. Amen.

10

What If?

But whoever has this world's goods, and sees his brother in need, and shuts up his heart from him, how does the love of God abide in him?

1 John 3:17

I grew up in the South, right in the middle of the Bible Belt, and I never ran across anyone who was willing to pay the cost. Out of all the memories I have of my interactions with Christians, I don't have one of the church ever giving to my family. If they had, perhaps things would have been a bit different at my house.

I grew up on a street called Free Avenue. You can't get much more ironic than that. We were far from free; we were enslaved by poverty. My mom shopped at the thrift store for all of our clothes. My dad made frequent stops at trash dumpsters behind several bargain stores near our neighborhood hoping to find Christmas gifts for us. Our yearly income was low enough to qualify for the welfare free lunch system in the public school. We were poor.

We were poor not because my dad was a deadbeat—not at all. My dad was a hard worker. He started a makeshift roofing company. He also purchased some repossessed trailers and fixed them up to rent. We had a family car and a couple of work trucks. To some of the people in our neighborhood I'm sure it looked like we had it made. But from what I remember, even when we had those things it seemed we were just going deeper in debt, ever widening the gap between us and any chance of a life of comfort and peace.

That financial tension created a lot of stress in my dad's life. He worked hard all day, and at night he drank away his sorrows with his roofing friends. Have you ever taken a slow walk through an impoverished neighborhood? Whiskey and beer are the antidotes for the heartsick feelings of the have-nots.

I told you earlier that when my dad got drunk, he got violent. I recall an incident when I was twelve years old that involved one of my dad's outbursts. After drinking a fifth of Wild Turkey, my dad lost it. I was in my room when I first noticed that he had been drinking. I heard yelling and screaming and the sound of pottery breaking against the wall. This was not a lazy stupor; my dad was on a rampage. It was early evening, and I decided I would just go ahead and go to bed. I didn't want to come out of my room for fear of the unknown. Then the worst sound I had heard that whole day sent my security senses alarming. It was my dad bellowing my name. "Tony!" he yelled. "You come here, boy, before I bust you up!" Throughout my childhood, hearing my dad's angry voice was so stressful for me that I often lost control of my bladder. He frightened me deeply.

He demanded that my sister and I sit on the couch. I couldn't see him because he was in another room in the house, but he was yelling so loudly it sounded like he was right next to my ear. When he came through the living room doorway, my heart sank into my stomach. He was holding his gun in his hand along with some bullets. It was a .38 Special revolver. He snapped something on the side of it and the empty bullet chamber slid out for loading.

Dad sat down on the couch opposite us, sweating and swearing. His hair, which was normally groomed sort of like Elvis's, was now wild and windblown. He looked up at us—one of his eyes covered by a lock of hair, the other crazed and bloodshot. My sister and I held each other's hands and sat silently. My heart was beating out of my chest.

Slowly loading the gun, he never looked at it; he just kept staring at us. As he loaded another bullet into its chamber, his lips snarled up and a drop of drool began its slow descent down his unshaven chin. "I'm going to kill your mother!" Our grip tightened, both of us knowing my dad never said something without following through with it. It seemed like I was sitting there forever, chilled by the thought that he might kill us first. I had heard a story in the news where a dad did that. Then just that quick, he jumped up and raced out of the house to find my mother. She was visiting with friends up the street. We sat motionless on that sofa, petrified with fear.

I wasn't sure how much time went by as I sat there thinking how I wished life was different for us. I did not hate my dad; I hated living with him. As I wondered what he was doing and if he would really kill her, I prayed for my mom. But I was unable to finish my prayer because of all the mental distractions. My mind couldn't stop replaying all the other terror-filled moments we had experienced during my father's drunken rages. The time at dinner when he punched me in the face for humming a song—something I did when I was nervous. And the time he turned over the dinner table on me and my sister. We lay there on the floor with gravy and beans and sharp pieces of broken plates around us as he vomited his hatred of his day all over us. And there were those six words that tore my soul apart: "I wish I'd never bought you!"

As I sat on that couch, my body began to shake. I looked at the clock. Two hours had passed and neither my sister nor I had moved. We were still clutching our hands and staring into midair. Our laps were stained with tears, and I thought I would come apart completely. When my mom's car pulled into the driveway, it was like the odd good part of a bad dream. We did not dare go outside. We didn't want to see my dad getting out of that car if he had killed her and traded vehicles. I heard the sound of the engine stopping, followed by a door opening and closing, then footsteps—light, close-together footsteps. It was my mom. My heart began to race. When the door opened and we saw her, in a freakish moment we didn't move and she didn't even acknowledge us. She looked fine physically, but she also looked like she had seen death face-to-face.

A few moments went by, and then she ordered us to go to bed. We did, not even mentioning that we'd had no dinner. I remember lying in my bed that night and hearing the door slam shut as my dad came back home. I did not sleep at all that night. The next day was Saturday. I remember the day because on Saturdays my dad would come home early from work, and then he and his drinking buddies would drink beer and hang out at the picnic table in our front yard. I stayed clear, which meant hiding in the backyard.

Every Saturday a minister by the name of Mr. Early came into our neighborhood to make sure I was going to ride his bus to church Sunday morning. I liked Mr. Early. I remember he played basketball with me in my backyard one day, on a dirt court with a netless rim on a warped plywood backboard that was held up by a wooden two-by-four. He was a good guy. But you know, sometimes being good can be the enemy of being your best. I never recall him stopping to talk with my dad. I'm sure he was aware of what the fathers in my neighborhood did to their children. My dad's drunkenness, our bruised bodies, and our undeniable poverty were in plain sight every time he came by. Yet he, a representative of the church of Jesus, never engaged my father's issues. My dad thought Jesus was a moot subject. He stayed enslaved to his sins, and I suffered the fallout.

Hear me out here. I'm not hating on Mr. Early. He was doing what he thought was right. Touch base with the kids on Saturday and have a big, successful busload of kids for church on Sunday. But what if . . . what if Mr. Early had engaged my dad? What if Mr. Early had paid the cost? How would it have been different in the Nolan home if Mr. Early had come over one day and said, "Bob, here's an envelope containing five hundred dollars. It's for your rent and utilities. I know the lack of money stresses you out. And when you get stressed, you drink and do things to your boy that makes you hate the man you never wanted to be. Here, Mr. Nolan, please take it. It's from Jesus. He loves you, Bob, and he cares deeply for you and your family."

I am weeping as I type this, thinking about what kind of relief could have come into our pain-filled world as a result of that one act. Would my dad have seen the relevance of Christianity? Would he have received Christ and gotten swallowed up in his love and shared that love with others? In a moment of conviction would he have said he was sorry for telling me he wished he had never bought me and that he loved me and was proud to be my dad? Those questions will never be answered. I could easily choose to let my heart become bitter and succumb to cold, stingy religion, thinking, "Nobody met my needs, so. . . ." But when I keep my ear pressed against the chest of God and hear his heartbeat for the hurting, the memories of my past compel me to help hurting people so they can find healing in Jesus.

Think about your own childhood. Are there people who intentionally made a positive difference in your life?

_____

_____

_____

Can you identify anyone in your life whom you could help with financial assistance? What obstacles are in your way? How does the person's need compare with the size of the obstacles?

_____

_____

_____

Fast-forward ten years and imagine the church becomes so well known for extravagant generosity that the news media gives a strong report about it on CNN. Write out a few of the responses you think might emerge from those who heard the report.

_____

_____

_____

Dear Lord Jesus, help me to reorder things within my heart so that I can be a hurt healer and help pay the cost in order that someone might taste of your goodness. Amen.

11

Focus!

Blessed are the pure in heart, for they shall see God.

Matthew 5:8

As Jesus tells the story of the Good Samaritan, he wants the people listening to know what it means to love and to have a clear picture of what it looks like to love others. Jesus uses him as an example of neighborly love, and what I find fascinating is that the Samaritan paints a perfect picture of who Jesus is. Jesus is our ultimate example of a hurt healer. Getting a good look at the Samaritan gives us great insight into Jesus, and Jesus brings a high-definition focus to what a hurt healer looks like.

Sometimes bringing things into focus can be difficult. Such was the case for me during a trip to a large shopping mall here in the greater Atlanta area where I live. My heart sank as I pulled into the Town Center Mall. It looked like every parking space that was close to the building was taken, and I would have to park 500 miles away in west Alabama. Without realizing that I was thinking out loud, I sarcastically snarled, "Town Sinner Mall!"

My wife snapped back, "What was that?"

Surprised that I had actually let my thoughts convert to vocal sounds that danced across my lips and into my wife's ears, I went into damage control. "I love Town Center Mall," I replied sheepishly.

Tammy snapped back, "No, you said Town *Sinner* Mall!"

It was my bad, so I kept quiet to avoid digging my way into a grave, which I was thinking might be a better option than shopping. I don't like malls; I don't like shopping. So I was thinking about driving to Alabama until Tammy found a spot wedged between two oversized SUVs. Now I was going to have to pull a Criss Angel or Brock Gill magic trick to fit into the parking space and get out of my car.

After we got out and walked 150 miles (why don't they have trolleys for guys with flat-screen TVs that play ESPN's *SportsCenter*?), we were finally inside. The smell of fresh chemicals invaded my nostrils, and I held my hand up over my nose to replace that smell with the Taco Bell scent that was still lingering from yesterday's lunch appointment. Nasty, I know, but I'm telling you it was better than the toxic fragrance of the garments hanging from the racks.

If that wasn't bad enough—*mall music*! I love good music, and that means I really hate bad music. I quickly used my hands to plug my ears and then began gagging because my nasal passage was now open. I fumbled back and forth trying to plug both ears and nose, and I finally found relief pressing my forefingers together to pinch my nose while spreading my fingers and shoving my thumbs into my ear canals. I looked up to see my wife gazing at me with sultry eyes of seduction as I stood there looking like a dork. The whole *opposites attract* thing causes her heart to flare when I act like a freak.

Okay, to tell the truth, she sneered and muttered something about childish men as she lost herself in an aisle of blouses and skirts. I quacked, "I'm gonna go find something cool to check out. Call me on my cell if you need me." She, of course, acted like she didn't know me.

I headed for the food court, hoping the Chick-fil-A guy would be offering samples. But I quickly became frustrated because the crowd wasn't moving at all. Tons of people had the halls congested to a standstill. My frustration meter was pegging on "about to go psycho" until I found out what the holdup was. One of those kiosks, the *wannabe stores* that are on carts in the middle of the hallway, had half the mall standing around looking at pictures.

I grunted until I saw why everybody had stopped. They were not your normal pictures. Sure they were in frames, but they didn't show anything but an unrecognizable rainbow of digitalized colors. The salesman was declaring to bystanders, however, that if you stared at the painting just right, a 3-D image would pop out at you. Tons of people were just standing there, tilting their heads and squinting their eyes, trying to see the hidden picture. I'm a sucker for a gimmick, so I found myself standing and squinting along with all the other goobers.

"Can you see the image?" the thief, I mean salesman, inquired. Startled, I had to back away a bit because he was standing three inches from my face and had invaded my line of vision of the painting.

Ribbing him a bit I replied, "Sure, buddy, I can see the picture. I just like staring at it for four hours along with all these other art lovers."

His voice changed into that of a weird fortune-teller, and he said, "I will share with you a secret to help you see the picture." With that, he popped a 3x5 white piece of paper in front of my nose (which I liked because it took the mall smell away for just a moment). Then with his voice even louder and sounding like he was casting an incantation on me, he said, "Here is how you can see the picture. Hold the card up to your nose and look at the card. As you look at the card, move the card away from your nose. As you move the card away from your nose, don't look at the card, look through the card! As you look through the card, *poof*, you see the picture!"

My eyes were popping from their sockets in response to his secret tip, and I asked, "Do you know that they make medication for people like you?"

He smiled and said, "Yes, but they don't make any that can help you see this picture," as he extended the piece of paper to me and gestured for me to give it a try.

It took a while. Tammy got in some serious shopping time. At first I couldn't get it. I was doing the "look through the card" bit, but everything remained blurry. It got really embarrassing because little children would come up and after just a few moments declare, "It's a fire ant! Do you see it, sir?"

To which I barked, "Don't talk to strangers! You better go find your momma, boy, before I feed you to the fire ants!"

But then in a victorious moment—rivaled only by the time I chewed gum and danced at the same time—it happened! I pulled the card away and *poof*, I saw the picture! The one I was getting a hemorrhaging tumor over turned out to be the Statue of Liberty. When I saw it, I saluted and started singing our national anthem, and the wacky sales guy asked me to leave. It was a memorable mall moment for me. I once was blind but now I can see!

I have discovered that spiritual principles are equally difficult to see. I often have a hard time seeing things in Scripture that Jesus wants me to understand. I pastor some of the leading artists in Christian music, and I admire their maturity and depth with God. Yet even they confess it's a common occurrence to struggle with clarity about spiritual truths. Anyone who is honest about his or her spirituality would make the same confession—that our eyes of faith often need a little assistance to focus in on a spiritual profundity. It is most encouraging, however, to know that just like the 3x5 card helped me to see the 3-D picture, God also gives us things to "look" at to help us bring the unseen into sight.

Typology provides this spiritual magnification. A type, as defined by theologian G. R. Osborne, is "a specific parallel between two historical entities."[1] My professor, Dr. John Pretlove at the Criswell Center in Biblical Studies, often said that types found in Scripture help bring into focus things God wants us to clearly see. It kind of breaks down like this: in the Bible, there are people, images, and events that paint a picture of the char-

> *Our eyes of faith often need a little assistance to focus in on a spiritual profundity.*

acter and activity of God as seen in his Son Jesus Christ. For instance, in Romans 5 we have Adam, the spreader of death to humanity, and then we have Christ, the giver of life to humanity. In chapter 21 of the book of Numbers, the bronze serpent that was raised in the air helped save the lives of all those who had been bitten by venomous snakes. In the Gospel of John, Jesus told Nicodemus that just as the bronze serpent was raised to give life, so he would be lifted up on a cross to save those who have been bitten by the serpent Satan. The exodus is a type of the activity of God in redemption. God brought his people out of bondage into the Promised Land, and in like manner, through Jesus God is freeing people from bondage to sin and preparing a place for us in heaven. Do you see it? Types help us get it. They are like the 3x5 card I used to see the 3-D picture.

In light of the definition of typology, I suggest that the Samaritan is actually a type of Jesus. In the classic use of typology, when we look at the life of this Samaritan, we see particular similarities to the work and ministry of Jesus Christ. His life points to the activity and ministry of the ultimate hurt healer who stands before them: Jesus from Nazareth.

Remember the three things the Samaritan did? In the next three chapters we will survey each one of those deeds and in so doing unveil this connection. I hope you find the exploration insightful. As I study this passage, I'm inspired to respond to Jesus's exhortation to "go and do likewise." One of my deepest desires in writing this book is that you will be too.

D E L V E

How would you define *focusing*, and how does your definition relate to following Jesus?

_____

_____

_____

Identify the top three things that help you to really focus on the things that truly matter.

_____

_____

_____

In what way is a *typology* significant in Scripture, and how might it help us spiritually?

_____

_____

_____

God, I must confess there are many things that blur my mind and hinder me from getting a clear picture of who you are. I need to see you in high-definition reality. Open my eyes through these next few chapters so I can behold you in all your glory. When this happens, I know I will be radically changed in supernatural ways. Amen.

12

Jesus Paused

Who, being in the form of God, did not consider it robbery
to be equal with God, but made Himself of no reputation,
taking the form of a bondservant, and coming in the like-
ness of men.

Philippians 2:6–7

Our Hurt Healer Samaritan put everything on pause to love
someone who needed it. A part of that pause included stepping out of his comfort zone and experiencing the fallout of
a sin-cursed world. Jesus Christ did the same.

The NIV translation makes it even clearer that the apostle
Paul is declaring one of the ultimate pauses Jesus made. He
writes that Jesus was the "very nature of God, [but] did not
consider equality with God something to be grasped" (Phil.
2:6 NIV). You are probably wondering how in the world I
think that has anything to do with pausing. Let's think about
it together.

Trying to spend time with friends is often difficult, but have you ever tried to get a moment with someone who is famous? It's a tough thing to get face time with people who are renowned. Some of them won't make time for you because they are full of themselves. I pray for those people because their fall from stardom will be long and hard.

But I actually have had the opportunity to pastor and minister to a lot of famous people. The ones I know are not mean and ugly toward others; they just are very, very busy. They have intense schedules because of all the demands on their lives. I'm thinking about the life of a St. Louis baseball player who is a friend of mine and a major supporter of my ministry: two-time MVP and World Series winner, Albert Pujols. He has a lot on his plate with a rigorous game schedule, disciplined training, endorsements, and the demands of being president of the Pujols Family Foundation. But something very touching and sort of magical happens when a guy like him puts everything in his life on pause and goes to the Dominican Republic to serve and minister to hurting, impoverished people. The faces of the people in the slums light up as Albert walks the streets and brings medicine and food for their families. He could be at home in Missouri soaking up the glamour and enjoying the luxuries that come with being a superstar. But instead, he lays it aside to care for others. That's big in my mind!

It's the kind of pausing Paul was trying to articulate about the life of Jesus. Think about it. According to the Gospel of John, Jesus has always been God and lived in the celestial wonders of heaven, running his Father's business. John 1:1 says, "In the beginning was the Word, and the Word was with God, and the Word was God."

There is no one who has ever been as famous as Jesus. All other great individuals, like Alexander the Great, the great Houdini, Tony the Tiger and his corn flakes, are not actually great. *Only God is great*, and his greatness is manifested in his Son, Jesus. This great Jesus was once in heaven ruling and reigning the universe, and then, "The Word became flesh and dwelt among us" (John 1:14). Jesus Christ, the most important being in existence, literally left the glory of his position and the environment of complete safety and serenity to come to this world and dwell among us.

Go with me in your mind's eye back to the moment when Jesus is telling the story of the Samaritan. Can you see the crowd, hear the noise, and feel the tension? Perhaps when Jesus refers to the Samaritan coming upon the injured man, his mind begins to remember what he left behind when he came to where we are. Jesus's brain replays memories of the celestial city and its sharp contrast to the world to which he

> *Jesus Christ, the most important being in existence, literally left the glory of his position to come to this world and dwell among us.*

has subjected himself. As the sun beats down on him, sweat trickles off his brow, causing him to recall how crisp, pleasant, and perfect the temperature is in his throne room.

I have a friend who lives in California. I have been to California several times on different preaching tours, but I would never live there because the threat of earthquakes and dropping off into the Pacific Ocean one day do not thrill me. My friend, on the other hand, gladly lives there along with millions of other people, and the reason they chance the "big one" is because of the beautiful weather. It is 75 to 80 degrees there year round. People love good weather. Well, it may be nice in California, but it's not heaven. To think Jesus left heaven and came to earth is like someone moving from California to the frigid mountains in Antarctica or to the blistering heat of Death Valley. But that's exactly what Jesus did. He came to where we are.

Meanwhile, back on the hot, dusty road, Jesus is still making his point to the lawyer. Standing there in his sandals, Jesus continues his story, and as he does, his foot shifts and a sharp pebble from the dirt road lodges between his toes, causing a pain to race up his leg. Plucking it free, Jesus holds it up to his eye and observes its roughness and sharp damaging edges. *Heaven has none of these—only gold, crystal clear water, and lush, green grass to snuggle your toes into and just say, ahhhhhh*, he muses.

That's another thing to think about, isn't it? Heaven is free from the curse; therefore, there are no briars, thorns, or cutting rocks that can hurt you. It's the perfect place to live. Yet Jesus left the perfectly manicured lawns of glory to come and hobble along our sticker-infested fields, craggy cliffs, and stony roadways.

That reminds me of going to my father-in-law's lake house in Keystone, Florida. It's a great place and a favorite for our family to visit. We love the white, sandy beach and the sparkling, clear lake, but we hate his front lawn. It is torture for the toes! On one occasion we pulled the car into the gravel driveway and my middle son, Wil, hopped out of the truck ready to stretch after the six-hour drive. After he jumped out, I noticed that he kept jumping around. He looked silly as his arms flailed left and right and his head spun in circles. I thought he was doing some kind of "we finally made it" celebration dance until I caught a glimpse of his face. He was in pain! With his eyes full of tears, he took one more hop back into the truck. He landed on his chest across the back seat with his feet stuck up in the air and screamed, *"Stickers!"* Stickers are little balls with hundreds of tiny, protruding needles that grow like a weed in your lawn. You don't really know they're there until you step on them and they pierce your skin and cut nerve endings that send you into orbit.

I would never have left heaven just knowing that the earth had stickers. But Jesus isn't like me. No, he is a true hurt healer through and through, and he came to where we are.

Allow your imagination to go with me back to the Bible again. I see Jesus speaking, and as he does, a mosquito lances his neck, dispensing a quick discomfort followed by an annoying itch that no amount of scratching can stop. He recalls the life he had before the incarnation where bugs and pain were never present. But now the Creator is willingly being hurt by his creation.

I don't like insects of any kind. They creep me out. When I was little, my family occasionally went on fishing outings at a place called Guyana in south Florida. The water hole was home to what my sister and I affectionately called the *flies from hell*. They were horseflies. I think they are called *horseflies* because they're the size of a small horse. When they land on you, if you survive the landing, it's followed by a bite that literally draws blood. They are vicious.

One time we decided to swim out into the deeper water. When we got out about one hundred yards from the shore, the horseflies showed up and started biting the tops of our heads. There must have been fifty of them. We began to scream and swim to the shore. But the flies kept dive bombing us and taking huge chunks out of our scalps.

I hatched a plan. I told my sister to swim under water to the shore. When we came up for air we splashed the surface, driving away the flies, took in a breath, went back under water, and swam farther toward shore. This was working until about my fourth time surfacing for air. I came up and did my splash, but one of those demon-possessed flies flew right into my mouth. I did not have time to react. I was taking in a quick, huge breath and plummeting under again to swim for my life. All I recall is choking under the water on what felt like a small animal that was buzzing, kicking, and scratching for his life as my esophagus constricted around him and drug him to the pit of my stomach. It was one of the most horrifying moments of my life. Like I said earlier, I hate insects. Just knowing that Jesus left the insect-free environment of heaven and subjected himself to their attacks on earth makes me shout his praises!

As we take another glance at Jesus speaking to the masses, I notice that all of a sudden the shouts of the crowd awaken him from his daydream about his homeland. Their angry faces and hostile words muster up a sigh from his chest as he vividly recalls that in heaven, every living creature reverently bows to him and shouts, "Holy! Holy! Holy!" As Paul says, he is God, but he did not hold on to the privileges and comforts God has. He released them and became a bondservant to help those in need.

I cannot speak for you, but what I know about the human experience tells me that not many of us would be willing to do the same. Sure, I've heard stories of amazing sacrifices made by people who were willing to do without so others could have. Those stories inspire me, and so it is with the story of Jesus as told in the Gospels. I am inspired by Jesus because I think about what I would do if I were him. I am not God nor have I ever claimed to be. And you should be glad that I'm not because I would not have left all of that comfort to come here and subject myself to so much pain and misery in order to save the world. Sorry to disappoint you. But it's that knowledge about myself that makes me so grateful for what Jesus did. He did it, people! He left it—the glory, the comfort, all of it—just so he could come to where we are. Jesus came here to our impoverished, sin-cursed world to minister to all of us who have been ambushed by the thief, Satan. It's sort of like watching one of your favorite DVDs and suddenly having a friend call with an important need. Most people would grab the remote and put the movie they were watching on pause so they could go attend to the need of their friend. That's what Jesus did with all his comforts and rights. He put them on pause to show some compassion to a world in need. That's something worthy of a lot of praise!

Think of something Jesus gave up in order to come here and heal our hurts. How would you have felt if you gave that up?

_____

_____

_____

What comforts do you think you need to give up so God can use you to show compassion to someone in need?

_____

_____

_____

What range of emotions strike you at the thought of having to give up something to show some love?

_____

_____

_____

O great God of heaven who came to earth, thank you for letting me see your example of how to love my neighbors. I rejoice and praise you for stepping out of heaven and subjecting yourself to this sin-cursed world so that I could be healed by your love. Amen.

13

Jesus Proved

For the joy that was set before Him [Jesus] endured the cross.

Hebrews 12:2

The Samaritan is far from the crowd and has to strain to hear each word Jesus is saying. A light wind is beginning to blow, causing the high wheatgrass to sway and clap its stems together, making it even more difficult to hear Jesus. But Jesus's words are clear: "He bandaged his wounds." Images flash in the Samaritan's mind as he vividly recalls that moment:

Startled by the sight of so much blood, the Samaritan initially is convinced the guy is dead and thinks about moving on. But in his mind he hears the voice of his mother and grandparents instructing him to serve and give and never walk past a person in need. Still, he finds himself wrestling with doing the right thing. He is human, and humans struggle when what they know they should do collides with what they don't want to do.

As this violent war rages within his spirit, his ear suddenly picks up another voice. It is faint, but the pain within it is deafening. As if exhaling his very last breath, the wounded man uses it to give what might have been his very last attempt at an SOS distress call.

Have you ever heard the cry of someone near death? Have you ever felt the gnawing absence of peace as you were overtaken with sudden horror from looking into the face of a limp human being in need of help? I've had an experience like that.

It happened at my father-in-law's lake house. (I told you it is a favorite place for the Nolans.) The lake was crystal clear and as smooth as glass. We were headed out to go wakeboarding and skiing when my wife, Tammy, thought she noticed something floating in the water. It concerned her because she had seen several children swimming in the water earlier. Something was wrong. She began telling her stepmother, Nan, what she feared as they began walking toward the spot in the water where an unidentifiable mass kept bobbing in and out of sight on the surface of the water. They picked up the pace, fearing the worst. What happened next will be forever etched into my memory.

Suddenly, Tammy's face contorted in horror. "Baby!" Nan yelled as she swiftly ran through the water to the floating body. Nan reached in and pulled out a little three-year-old boy. He lay lifeless across her arms. She dashed to the shore and began CPR. Tammy was screaming, and the parents, who were nearby, raced to the boy. An uncle of the child was also there, and he assisted Nan with CPR. The dad, who was on the beach and had been assigned the responsibility of watching the children, raced over to help. I immediately ordered my sister-in-law to take my three children up to the house and asked them to begin praying. And then I immediately began praying myself. I asked the Lord God of heaven to save the precious child's life. I thought, *What glory could he get out of a little child dying?* I admit I did not know what to pray, but honestly, when you are faced with a moment like that, it is as if God is pleading through you to himself. With my hands stretched out high to the heavens and with my voice loud, I began just pleading for God to have mercy on the child.

The boy was a dark blue color; he had been under for a while. Tammy had first seen the children playing in the water eight to ten minutes before, but there was no way to know exactly when he had gone under. As they lay him on the beach, the boy did not move. To protect the child's privacy, we will call him Kyle. I watched the dad cry out loud: "Kyle, oh Kyle, please oh my God, Kyle!" And then I watched that dad take his hands and dig them into the wet sand, and as he raked them along he just kept crying, "What have I done? What have I done?"

He had been drinking alcohol and in his stupor had gotten distracted from watching Kyle and his siblings swim. As the uncle and Nan worked on the boy, he shook violently and expelled a dark liquid from his mouth and nose. We had hope! And then I heard it. Even as I write this I am crying thinking about what I heard. The tiny little child's eyes rolled back into his head, his lips quivered, and he let out a hissing sound mingled with a very low gurgle. They rolled Kyle onto his side to try to clear out his passages. More of the lake water purged from his lungs and stomach.

With his eyes rolled back and his little fingers reaching blindly for anything to cling to, he made the noise again. It was not intelligible, but everyone could tell he was struggling to live. I began to weep openly. I had never seen a child suffer so.

When the paramedics arrived, Kyle was still limp and lifeless. Hearing his groan, they lifted him and the weight of his head caused it to roll forward. My heart sank at the sight of the child's helplessness. The medics secured him to a board and rushed him off in an ambulance to a nearby helicopter. Moments later, we watched as a helicopter flew above the tree line and raced away to the nearest hospital. We sat on the beach stunned and drained from the pain and fear of seeing a child dying before our very eyes.

Thankfully, Kyle lived. But the memory of that heartbreaking day will never be erased from my mind.

Something moves you deeply when you encounter a fellow human being whose life is on the line. And that's the situation in which our Samaritan friend found himself. Let's go once again to the scene of the tragedy.

Upon hearing the man's gasp, the Samaritan shouts, "He's alive!" The Samaritan's disposition alters radically, transforming from a relaxed, slow-paced traveler to an intense emergency trauma doctor. Frantically he tears a foot-long strip off his cloak and uses it as a tourniquet on the victim's bleeding arm. The depth of the gash reveals that the thieves had punctured a main vein, and he is near bleeding out. With no regard to the cost of the garment he is wearing, he tears another large piece off and begins pushing it into the large laceration while pouring wine in to help clean the wound. There is so much blood. Thick pools of it stain the road, and clots of it cover the man's head and body.

As he washes the man's face, the Samaritan is frozen in shock. He stops tightening the tunic and halts cleaning the wound. He recognizes the victim. He is the bully who beat him up almost every day of his childhood for being a Samaritan. Thoughts of those painful altercations and hatred surge within him.

The Samaritan's mother taught him to view every hurting person as if he or she is his closest and most loved friend or family member. Her voice overpowers his anger.

> "Care for him as if he were me." He shakes his head to clear his mind. And with the determination of an Army medic tending to the wounds of an enemy combatant, he rolls up his sleeves.

The Samaritan proved he cared for the hurting man, and in so doing he provided a picture of how Jesus proved he cares for humanity. When people suffer, they are prone to question whether God cares for them. But if you look at the life and ministry of Jesus Christ as shown in the Scriptures, his compassion is obvious.

The Samaritan proved he cared for the hurting man, and in so doing he provided a picture of how Jesus proved he cares for humanity.

As Jesus tells the listening throng that the Samaritan bandaged up the hurting man's wounds, I imagine Jesus thinking to himself, *I am here to do the same for you.* Jesus may have remembered standing before a different crowd, this time assembled in a synagogue where he stood and quoted the prophet Isaiah:

> The Spirit of the LORD is upon Me,
> Because He has anointed Me
> To preach the gospel to the poor;
> He has sent Me to heal the brokenhearted,
> To proclaim liberty to the captives
> And recovery of sight to the blind,
> To set at liberty those who are oppressed;
> To proclaim the acceptable year of the LORD.
>
> Luke 4:18–19

After speaking, Jesus sat down and proclaimed that these words were being fulfilled right before their very eyes. Talk about stirring up the crowd! Jesus was saying he was the Messiah who had come to minister to the world. Do you see what he said he would be doing? Along with preaching the gospel and proclaiming the acceptable year of the Lord, Jesus said he was here to care. He came to heal brokenhearted people, set captive people free, and give sight to the spiritually blind. Jesus came to care just like the Samaritan did.

In the Samaritan story I have painted a hypothetical situation of the wounded man being a bully who tormented the Samaritan. But in the story about Jesus, I have taken no creative license. Instead, there is only the glory and awesomeness of Jesus coming down to earth and dying for us—the very ones who would kill him.

> **Jesus willingly embraced the cruel torture of crucifixion in order to heal the bleeding, sinful wounds of our souls.**

The Bible says he came unto his own and his own did not receive him. His creation turned on him and bullied him. Yet with unflinching compassion he willingly embraced the cruel torture of crucifixion in order to heal the bleeding, sinful wounds of our souls. We were drowning in the sea of a sin-cursed world. Christ picked us up through the cross. He breathed life into our suffocating spiritual lungs and resuscitated our lifeless bodies. Jesus proved he cares.

DELVE

Humans struggle when what we know we should do collides with what we don't want to do. Describe in detail a moment when you were faced with this great collision. What did you do?

_____

_____

_____

Have you engaged a person in need? If not, why? If so, what was the defining factor that caused you to get involved?

_____

_____

_____

Jesus came and died for you and me and the very ones who killed him. In what way does that vanquish any questions in your mind that Jesus cares?

_____

_____

_____

Lord of heaven and earth, I stand in awe of your caring touch. No words describe the gratitude I have for the death you died in the place of those who butchered you on the cross. Help me to feel for others. I pray that your power will win the battle when I don't want to do what I know I should do. Amen.

14

Jesus Paid

For God so loved the world that He gave His only begotten Son.

John 3:16

I get thousands of emails from people who identify with my painful childhood, asking my opinion about how to get over the past and move toward a healthier future. One of the most frequently asked questions is, "What hurt you the most in your painful childhood experience?" Many assume it was the beatings from my dad. But those were not the worst. I wore several pairs of underwear and my pajamas under my jeans to soften the blows. Some people think it had to be being poor. But our poverty was manageable through my skills as a thief. The thing that hurt me the most was not hearing three words that every boy longs to hear from his father: "I love you." I never heard those words from him. I heard the exact opposite. My dad regularly told me that he wished he had never bought me. Those words crushed me.

I will never forget the first time my dad said that to me. I was having a bad day at school. I had gotten into a fight with another fifth grader who made fun of my hand-me-down shoes my mom picked up at the thrift store. He poked fun and called me names. As my other classmates joined in with vicious laughter, I remember sinking in my spirit and wishing I could turn invisible. I had a vivid imagination that enabled me to soar with Superman over the playground and avoid homework with stealth like Batman. But the ability to spontaneously vanish eluded me in real life. My head hung low as I walked home from school.

It was a very cold day for Florida. Trees bent and swayed from the blustery fall wind. The cold air sent chills across my skin, reminding me of the frigid comments made by my classmates. Just then I thought of a way I could vanish. I started running home thinking that once I got there I would lock my door, never to be seen by anybody again for the rest of the day.

I arrived home, flung open the door, and tossed my book bag on the floor. And as I turned into the kitchen for a cookie and some milk, I crashed into my dad. He yelled, "Get changed. You're coming to work with me. I'm clearing a yard, and I want you to rake up the pine needles." My face frowned and my shoulders did too. He barked out, "What the h— is wrong with you, boy?"

I started to cry, and he called me a "silly fag"—one of his favorite verbal grenades. Tears welled up. I wanted to tell him about the other boys who were picking on me at school. But there was no way I could let him know how much it hurt me, because according to him, if your emotions weakened due to the actions of others, it meant you were not a man. I stuttered, "I—I—I don't want to—to go. I had—had a b-b-b-bad day."

His eyes met mine, and I cowered like a scorned dog as he yelled, "You're not my son! My son would want to work!" His words ripped open the wounds my classmates had caused earlier, and my soul began to bleed again. Then he screamed, "Is this all two hundred dollars got me?" At first I did not understand. *Was he upset because he purchased some tool that didn't work? What did he mean?* Then he made it clear and personal. "I wish I'd never bought you!"

My dad had just told me I was worthless. The sound of shattering glass filled the air. Nothing in the house was broken. Dad had not thrown a vase or plate. It was my heart crashing on the floor of my hardened spirit. I wanted to run back to school and just sit and take the abuse of my classmates forever. Anything would be better than hearing my dad tell me I was worthless. I had always struggled with my self-worth, having had so much trauma as an orphan. Now the struggle was over. I lost. There was no need to fight to find worth anymore because my father was telling me I had none. He was so dissatisfied with me that he regretted ever adopting me.

"Then take me back!" I screamed. With my hand over my mouth, surprised that I had spoken my thoughts out loud, I prepared for the counterattack from my father. He stood there for a split second and then quickly pulled off his belt. I knew what was coming, so I instinctively turned to run and dodge the coming blows. I was too slow; the belt lanced across my arms. I reeled in pain. I knew more would follow, so I sank to the ground. The next one went across my back, followed by another over my legs.

As I lay bent into a ball with my eyes closed tight, he wielded two more stinging blows across my head and neck. "Get your — up off that floor and into my truck, boy!" With my eyes still shut, I lay there anticipating more hits. Then I heard the sound of his belt sliding across fabric through the loops in the waist of his pants. The beating was over, but the hurt had only begun.

I sat in the truck and stared out the window as we raced up the road to go work on the yard. A single leaf that was dancing along the gusty wind summoned jealousy in my heart as

I imagined it singing, "I am free, I am free, wouldn't you like to be like me?" I so wanted to be free like that, but instead I was imprisoned by worthlessness. Parts of my body were radiating with pain. I noticed my hand had a red mark across it, evidence of an encounter with my father's leather belt. My reflection in the side rearview mirror revealed I had another one on the side of my face. The wounds were hurting, but nothing hurt as much as my heart did. "I wish I'd never bought you," echoed through my mind as if in cadence with the surges of pain from the welts on my body.

The wounds were hurting, but nothing hurt as much as my heart did.

I was worthless, and there is no way to describe how painful that thought was for me. I lived—well, not really; it was more like existing—locked in that emotional prison for most of my life. Then one day I met the Hurt Healer.

On February 24, 1989, I woke up with a hangover and knocked over a half-empty beer can that was sitting on my nightstand. I lit a cigarette and rubbed my temples, seeking relief from my pounding head. Bright rays of sunshine were squeezing through the partially closed window blinds and streaking across my bedroom wall. Squinting at their presence, I began to get furious. I wasn't angry at the sun; I was mad because I was still alive.

The night before I had tried to drink myself to death, and I had failed again. I wrestled with suicide. I had many friends who had succeeded in death by the use of alcohol. One of them climbed a tree and pulled a case of beer up with a rope. As he drank, he tied the rope onto the tree limb he was sitting on and tied the other end around his neck. He kept drinking until he lost the ability to stay up in the tree. When he fell he hanged himself.

I wanted to do something like that. Every day those hateful words of my father, "I wish I'd never bought you!" bounced around in my head like a ball in a pinball machine. Inhaling the Marlboro Light, I summoned up my death-wish battle cry and determined to succeed that day.

At seven o'clock that night, I ended up in a place I never thought I would be—a Bible study. My stepbrother had become a Christian, and he kept inviting me to church. Every time he asked, I told him *no*. On this day when he called and asked, I tried to give him my normal reply, but somehow *yes* came out of my mouth. I had been drinking a lot of beer already, so I guess I slipped up. It proved to be a lot better than slipping out of a tree with a rope around my neck.

I don't remember a lot of the first part of the night because I walked into the church stoned on pot and loopy from beer. I really didn't even listen. As a child I had heard about Jesus. I knew he died on a cross, was buried, and rose again. But I just sat there drowning in my father's verbal vomit. I do recall that the Christians who had gathered for the Bible study drank a lot of coffee, and before long I was borderline sober.

When it was over, my stepbrother took me home, and as we sat in his truck in the driveway, he shared the gospel with me. He started off by reading several Scripture verses that highlighted my sin. I already knew I was a bad person; I had been told all my life that I was trouble and a pain. Hearing those Scriptures just affirmed what everyone said about me and gave me another reason to kill myself.

I started to get out of the truck, determined to fulfill my death wish. And then something enchanting and supernatural happened. Like a conversation that gets interrupted, God butted in, and my father's voice began to fade as God screamed through the madness with a whisper and lovingly said, "Tony, your adoptive father discouraged you by telling you he wished he had never bought you. Oh Tony, I have never regretted purchasing you with the priceless blood of my Son. I love you, Tony. Let me be your heavenly Father."

That night I confessed my sins to God, placed my childlike faith in Jesus, and was swallowed up by the love of God. He picked my bent-out-of-shape life up off the sin-cursed road, and I could feel the therapeutic power of God's mercy, grace, and love flowing through all the deep wounds of my soul. My spirit awakened to new life!

Like the Samaritan who paid a cost to help a hurting person, Jesus paid a price to mend my hurting soul. He gave his blood. He gave his life. I was awestruck and humbled to be awakened to the reality that I was so valuable to God that he gave the life of his Son to adopt me into his heavenly family.

> *I was so valuable to God that he gave the life of his Son to adopt me into his heavenly family.*

He has extended this same love to you and every hurting heart in the world. Humanity is so treasured and valued by God that he paid an infinite cost to redeem our souls.

D E L V E

Why do you think it means so much for the human heart to be told it is loved?

_____

_____

_____

Think of people you know who are bent out of shape. Describe how their lives would be altered if they became convinced that God has never regretted purchasing them with the priceless blood of his Son.

_____

_____

_____

Does this chapter make you grateful for salvation? Take a few minutes and write an email to God. Pour out your heart to him about how grateful you are that he paid the ultimate price of his life to adopt you into his family. Save the email as a draft. Go back from time to time and read that email out loud to God in your prayer time.

If you have never been saved and would like to be, just do what I did that night and by faith agree with God that you are a sinner. Don't try to figure salvation out, just accept it by faith. Call out the name of the Lord Jesus, surrender your life to his leadership, and live the rest of your life in thankfulness for the price he paid to forgive you. Then email me at tony@tonynolan.org and let me know about your conversion.

Jesus, I am stunned by the price you paid to provide salvation for my soul. A simple thank you *does not adequately express the profound gratitude that I have in my heart. Therefore, I won't let it be mere words, but may my choices, thoughts, and worship confirm my confession of thanks every day. In the name of the Father and the Son and the Holy Spirit, amen.*

PART 2

SHOWINGJESUS

15

Do Likewise

For as the body without the spirit is dead, so faith without
works is dead also.

James 2:26

I want to start this chapter by asking you a very serious question: Is there anything that you read in the last three chapters
about Jesus's life that caused you to think he sucks? If you are
a thinking person and have even a small amount of gratitude
for what he did for you, then your answer has to be, "No!"
Jesus said that when you look at him, you see the Father.
Therefore, what we know about God says that he doesn't
suck. He paused for compassion, proved he cared, and paid
the cost. God is unquestionably compassionate, beautifully
kind, and unselfishly generous.

Let me remind you, however, that many non-Christians
think Jesus does suck. How can they say such a thing after
what we just read about him? We need to remember that
they, for the most part, don't read the Bible or Christian
writings. They read the fine print found in the chapters of

our everyday lives as we live, play, and work with them. You see, their problem isn't with the God we *know*; they don't like the God we *show*. That's the fallout that occurs when the God we know is not the God we show.

Jesus is well aware of the breakdown, and I think it's one of the reasons he took the time to address the lawyer and tell the story about the Good Samaritan. Jesus desires to see a life change happen in us so that a life change can happen in others who need him. I think that's one of the main reasons Jesus concludes the story with the question, "Which of these three do you think was [a] neighbor to him who fell among thieves?" The answer to the question was really a no-brainer because the correct reply instantly shot back from the lawyer, "He who showed mercy on him." And then came the exhortation that needs to be embraced with more fervor today than ever before, as Jesus said, "Go and do likewise" (Luke 10:36–37).

As I listen to those words, "Go and do likewise," I find my imagination drifting back to the scene of Jesus surrounded by a swarm of people. Their hearts were already dizzy from riding in the front row of the emotional roller coaster Jesus just took them on through his gripping story. Although the crowd was diverse, most of their hearts were in agreement with the way they felt about the priest, Levite, and Samaritan. But if we could see into their hearts now through some sort of infrared, Special Forces recon glasses that could detect emotional variations, it would show every heart moving in its own unique direction. This fragmentation of heart unison came as a result of Jesus getting personal with the story.

The reason they had gathered in the first place was to see Jesus the demon slayer put the lawyer in his place. Now they stood with eyes wide, mouths dropped, and hearts racing because Jesus had just put *them* in their place. He not only exposed the priest and Levite, but he also exposed their own propensity to fail in the area of loving their neighbor. The hurtful heretics were obviously guilty of cruel selfishness, but everyone listening to Jesus was also guilty.

You may be questioning me here, thinking I am misjudging the crowd. Actually we are all guilty of being self-absorbed. Before you grab your cloak of righteousness and defend yourself, I encourage you to consider Jesus's words used in the second commandment. Have you ever noticed it before? "Love your neighbor as your*self*" (Matt. 19:19, italics added). Jesus was so sure of each person's propensity to be wrapped up in his or her own interests, wants, desires, and ambitions that he used our selfishness to illustrate and leverage his exhortation to love others. Wow! I'm going to have to concede and raise my hand in confession and say, "Guilty."

This kind of rebuke is not always well received. But the people listening to Jesus did, in fact, embrace it. So have billions of other people over the two-thousand-year span since our Lord first spoke those words in the presence of the hostile crowd. Christianity throughout the ages has been marked by people who selflessly love their neighbors. How did Jesus get people to buy into being neighbor-loving hurt healers? I think it's because he inspired them to do it through his own example. We read in the last three chapters that Jesus practiced what he preached. He didn't ask his followers to do something that he himself was not willing to do, and that kind of leadership inspires radical *follow*-ship.

At a conference some nineteen years ago, I heard a preacher by the name of Richard Lee tell a story that moved my heart. It was a very cool story that involved kings, castles, and kingdoms. It totally illustrates the principle I'm talking about here, where Jesus is inspiring his followers to radical follow-ship. I want to tell it to you, but I'm going to tell it differently from the way I heard it. I want to tell it the way my mind has interpreted and meditated on it for over nineteen years.

Many years ago, when the world was divided by kingdoms and castles, a war broke out between two kingdoms. On the morning of the battle, the air was thick with a chilly wetness. An eerie fog hovered and curved along the grassy hills of the battlefield. The armies were separated across the great divide of the field. Scared boys posing as unconquerable men summoned courage as they stood assessing the protection they might attain within their ironclad armor. Banners whipping in the wind in cadence with the powerful snorts of battle horses provided the battle's musical score. A prayer was lifted, followed by a trumpet blast, and the war was on. The thunder of running horses united with a thousand advancing warriors exploded in every ear. Thoughts of fighting maneuvers colliding with memories of babies and wives left back home whirled within the knights' minds. Steel swords clashed with steel shields. Thousands of men fell to their death with gurgled screams as they choked on their own blood.

Only one king had chosen to fight alongside his army. As he was shielding one of his knights from the blow of a double-edged axe, he was hit across the neck and mortally wounded. He fell to the ground as ten of his knights swarmed around him swinging their swords and spears wildly, keeping back any approaching foe.

His armor bearer ran to his aid. Seeing the massive blood loss, he calmly asked his king for the honor of serving him once more before his death. He pledged, "O gracious and courageous king, grant me this day the honor of serving thee once more!" His tears rolled off his face and onto the bloody cheeks of his beloved king.

Although gasping for air through his lacerated larynx, the king replied with dignity, "There is but one thing you can do for your king. Go before me into the afterworld and tell them the king is coming!" Without hesitation the armor bearer swiftly unsheathed his sword and drove it hard through his own heart. He slowly fell across the chest of the king, who placed his hand on the loyal servant's chilled brow and then gently smiled and breathed his last.

When I hear King Jesus say, "Go and do likewise," I think of this story. Jesus is not asking us to do something he was not willing to do himself. He led by example. He came to this earth and did battle alongside us against the forces of evil. Jesus suffered mortal wounds through the cross. When I look at Jesus and think of all that he did for me, I am inspired by his life and example. I find myself weeping and asking like the armor bearer, "What might I do to serve you, King?" His answer is, "Go and do likewise." May we be an army of hurt healers who, without hesitation, take the sword of the Spirit, drive it through our self-centered hearts, and live to tell this world the King is coming!

Jesus's exhortation to "do likewise" has been adhered to for a long time. But it appears that with so many people in our culture who have an unfavorable impression of Jesus, we are on the cusp of all-out national rejection of Jesus. Don't you think that something must be done now? But what? The Good Samaritan story tells us.

Have you ever been watching TV and your program is interrupted by an urgent news flash? Jesus's story acts in the same way. We interrupt your normal Christian living to bring you this word from God, and that message is: *be like Jesus*.

For years, many of those in the Christian culture in America have been wearing little bracelets bearing the letters *WWJD*. Those four letters stand for *What Would Jesus Do?* A Christian band in the nineties called Big Tent Revival wrote a song titled "What Would Jesus Do," making the slogan and bracelets a national craze. The message started showing up everywhere. It was in Wal-Mart on the impulse buyers' rack, on arms of just about every student in every church in the U.S., and even on the cover of *Sports Illustrated* gracing the wrist of the famed late golfer Payne Stewart.

Now hear me out. I am not hating on those who have worn or are currently wearing the bracelets. I just want to say something to screw you up and get you to open your eyes and heart. What if we moved beyond merely *considering* what Jesus would do and started *copying* what he did? Perhaps we should change one letter in the *WWJD* phenomenon. Let's make it *DWJD*, which stands for *Do What Jesus Did*! I think that was the point Jesus was making that hot day thousands of years ago when he closed out his masterful story by saying, "Go and do likewise." He never asked the crowd, "What would the Samaritan do?" Instead he asked, "What did he do?" Then he challenged us deeply and said, "Go and do likewise."

Let's think back to when Jesus was addressing the subdued crowd. Remember how each person's heart was responding differently to Christ's exhortation? I'd like to know what Mr. Hurting was thinking. Perhaps a smile spanned his busted lips as he reflected on the day death met its match through the love of a hurt healer. I imagine his black-and-blue eyes began to swell with moisture. And when his memory of the help he had received mingled with the awareness that the breath he just took would not have been possible if that Samaritan had not proved he cared, tears uncontrollably drenched his face. As Jesus's words ricocheted off every contour of his heart, overtaken with emotion his quivering lips whispered, "This pain-filled world would be a better place if it were inhabited with more people like him."

I think so too. But being a hurt healer is not just about making this world a better place. There is a greater goal for the hurt healer.

D E L V E

Jesus closed his story with, "Go and do likewise." Most people don't go and do likewise because they experience hesitations that arise from everyday life. What are some hesitations in your life?

_____

_____

_____

Write down your reaction to the story of the fighting kingdoms and the act of the armor bearer.

_____

_____

_____

What is it going to look like for you to take the sword of God's Word and attack those hesitations you listed in the first question?

_____

_____

_____

Take a moment and articulate the way you see the difference between the two statements, "What would Jesus do?" and "Do what Jesus did."

_____

_____

_____

Precious Savior, when I look at the example you left
me to follow—how you came and did battle with
Satan, and you took the fall for us on the cross—I am
inspired! Courage, love, and faith awaken within me,
and I will let the sword of the Spirit slash through
the dark stuff of my heart that keeps me from being
all that I need to be. I unapologetically proclaim to
this world that you, my King, are coming! Amen.

16

Divine Deeds

For what will it profit a man if he gains the whole world, and
loses his own soul?

Mark 8:36

Buck "Ballistic" Burney is my father-in-law. It's my claim
to fame. He is a very cool man and one of my best friends.
God has used him to mend a lot of hurts that I had in my
heart from my father. He personifies being a hurt healer, and
he has taught me that the greatest exercise of the heart is to
bend down and pick someone up.

Just about everything about him is cool, but one thing
about my father-in-law that is really super cool is his job.
He's a fighter pilot! He flew F-16 and F-15 jets and served
as commander of the Air Force base in Homestead, Florida.
He recently retired and now speaks to thousands of church
and corporate leaders through his "Mission on Target" motivational enterprise. He has a really cool life.

It should be noted, however, that he has never taken me flying in a jet. (He took Dr. John Maxwell up, but I'm not bitter.) But he did take me to a state-of-the-art simulator that was off the hook and bad to the bone. It was a very exciting and wonderful experience.

I love the whole fighter pilot culture. They are not just *multitask oriented*, they are *multitask executors*. When your office desk is a cockpit that soars over 50,000 feet high, faster than the speed of sound, while your hand is on a trigger that launches missiles, you have to be a precise multitask executor. I love to see execution happen with excellence. When these guys set out to accomplish a mission, it is done with every part of the organization at the top of their game.

One of the things his world has taught me has to do with the discipline of briefing and debriefing missions. Before the squadron executes a mission, they brief it. They go over every functional objective that is necessary to pull off the mission so that every team member knows exactly what they are to do and when they are to do it. Everybody is dialed in because if they fail, someone could die. It is serious and dangerous work.

Once the pilots accomplish their mission, they debrief. The team meets together and rewinds the mission. They review every task and evaluate the effectiveness of each action. As a rule, they hone in on everything that actually contributed to the success of the mission. When those things are defined, the team takes note and makes sure that they implement those strategies in future missions. But they also scrutinize and articulate any activity that did not contribute to the success of the mission. And as a rule, they make sure that they never, ever spend any energy on those things again. I love that kind of thinking. It keeps the organization lean and yields the most return on the energy invested in the mission.

Having my father-in-law in my life has caused me to begin thinking this way about almost everything. It gets a little squirrelly when I find myself briefing and debriefing about eating my breakfast cereal or brushing my teeth, but it's a great way to think when it comes to the mission of a hurt healer.

For many years the church has defined a Good Samaritan as one who simply spares people from catastrophes. Good Sams are characterized by feeding the hungry, paying someone's rent, bringing relief to hurricane victims, and doing other humanitarian deeds. When I stop and debrief this kind of Samaritan activity while wearing my fighter pilot thinking cap, however, I start dialing in on the bigger picture. My mind tells me that our time on earth is very short. Therefore, we not only need to spare people from a catastrophe, we need to prepare them for eternity.

We not only need to spare people from a catastrophe, we need to prepare them for eternity.

Let's debrief our culture's current humanitarian emphasis. One of the popular Samaritan movements sweeping our nation is *random acts of kindness*. The movement is so pervasive that it made it onto the big screen in the movie *Evan Almighty*. The movie is about a man in modern America who is called by God to build an ark in order to save a community from a flood that is going to occur from a defective river dam. In one scene, God (played by Morgan Freeman) writes the word ARK in the sand. He then tells Evan Baxter (played by Steve Carell) that the world would be a better place if everybody would do one act of random kindness.

This idea has gotten a lot of traction in our society. But my fighter pilot thinking tells me this movement has a little of the *WWJD* thing going on with it. It sounds good but falls a bit short and needs a little tweaking to be eternally effective. Did you catch that? I said, for it to be *eternally* effective.

Here is how random acts of kindness play out. It starts with someone in need. Let's say the person is starving and needs something to eat. A group of caring and helpful people hear about it and then respond by providing some nutritional food. After the individual is fed, the group leaves and heads home. Feeding the person was a good thing to do. But I want to propose to you that the *good* thing to do can often be the enemy of the *best* thing to do.

Do you remember my mentioning Dr. Maxwell earlier? Dr. Maxwell told a story at a leadership conference I attended that gives some insight about good versus best. As I often do, I'm going to tell the story to you as I saw it within my imagination.

The story is about a lighthouse positioned along Maine's treacherous northern shoreline. Seafarers' lives were protected by the weathered little cottage and its towering black-and-white striped beacon. The light within it was produced by a large, oil-burning wick, surrounded by a huge magnification lens. Its intense radiant beam could be seen by sailors from miles away as it rotated and stretched across the dark night sky.

The lighthouse keeper was a unique figure of a man. He was short and had a chubby, wrinkled face that held a contagious smile. Most people thought of him as one of Santa's elves who was entrusted with the task of caring for seamen. All of the residents on the island were very fond of him. His heart was kind, and he was known for his hospitality and generosity. Neighbors often heard him whistle while he worked doing the only job he had ever loved—keeping the beacon lit.

One day a lady suffering from a mild chill came by needing some oil for heat. He wanted her to be comfortable, so he gave her some oil. A farmer also came by in need of some oil to fuel his tractor. The lighthouse keeper gladly retrieved a large amount from his supply and gave him what he needed. Several other people who also needed oil for various reasons came by that week. Out of the kindness of his heart he gave oil to all of them.

Then it happened. A terrible storm swept across the coastal region. Great waves crashed on the jagged cliffs as gusty winds lifted away anything on the beaches that wasn't secured. The lighthouse keeper went to the top of the lighthouse to see if he could tell if any ships were caught out in the storm. Once he got into the upper room, he mused as to how it always looked like the inside of a massive lantern. The burning wick surrounded by a large, rotating, crystal lens set within a 360-degree room of glass windows was his favorite perch to view the ocean's activity. As he shielded his eyes from the light coming through the lens, he squinted and scanned the churning horizon. He saw several bow lights going in and out of sight as they bobbed up and down on the waves. He smiled and was at rest knowing that his light was keeping them safe from danger.

As he sipped a warm, cozy cup of coffee, he prepared for a long night. Then the unthinkable happened. The flame in the grand light began to dim. He quickly ran to troubleshoot and fix the problem. Had he trimmed the wick too short? He turned a crank to raise the wick, but it did nothing. He stared as the small, flickering flame danced along the charred edge of the wick, and in an instant the room became saturated with darkness. His mind raced, and he shouted out loud, "Oil!" It was out of oil.

As his heart sank, his mind began to replay all the moments of the week when his visitors came by in need. He raced down the stairs and hurried into the supply room to check the oil drum. He kicked the container, and the hollow sound that echoed throughout the musty cottage basement confirmed his fears. He was out of oil. There was nowhere to go for more and nothing he could do, though try as he might, to relight the wick. The night did, in fact, prove to be long. It was one of the longest nights of his life, and it proved to be the last night in the lives of the sailors stranded out in the horrors of the turbulent deep waters and rocky shore. When morning came, the beach looked like a battlefield laden with the corpses of those who had fought for their lives. Hundreds of sailors had died as their ships were dashed against the rocky shore.

You see, the lighthouse keeper did good acts to those in need of oil, but it was at the expense of what was best for those who were in need of light. Do you see it? The good can be the enemy of the best. In like manner, I think it is good to do a random act of kindness, but I suggest that it would be best to do a Deliberate Divine Deed.

It is good to do a random act of kindness, but it would be best to do a Deliberate Divine Deed.

What is a Deliberate Divine Deed? It is the trademark of a hurt healer. Deliberate Divine Deeds are much like random acts of kindness but taken a step further. They start with a physical need, such as a person in need of food. A hurt healer becomes aware of the need and responds by providing great food. But before leaving after meeting the physical need, the hurt healer takes the opportunity to make sure that the person's greatest need is attended to—and that's the condition of his or her soul.

You see, hurt healers are Christians who embrace loving their neighbor to the fullest extent. How can we say that we have loved our neighbors if we don't share with them the greatest act of love? That great act of love is Jesus Christ dying on the cross to satisfy the greatest need of our souls—salvation. God forbid that we feed a hungry man and he dies and goes to hell on a full stomach. You may question whether that ever really happens. I can't say for sure, but I'm haunted by the idea that it will if all Christians do is meet physical needs without ever dialing in on the condition of the person's soul.

Take a few minutes and try to define what it means to *brief* and *debrief.*

_____

_____

_____

How would this discipline of briefing and debriefing help you be a better servant of God?

_____

_____

_____

In what specific way do you see a Deliberate Divine Deed being more effective in an individual's life than a random act of kindness?

_____

_____

_____

How did your mind and heart respond to the very last paragraph of this chapter?

_____

_____

_____

Mighty Savior Jesus, I confess that random acts fall short. Life is brief and our time on earth is short, so please help me be deliberate in sharing the Good News when I do a good deed. I desire to be a hurt healer who deeply and sincerely cares about people's eternal destination. Amen.

17

Forever Somewhere

And being in torments in Hades, he lifted up his eyes and saw
Abraham afar off, and Lazarus in his bosom.

Luke 16:23

It was the end of an uneventful day, but it would prove to be
an unusually eventful night. The evening air was cold—the
kind of cold where stepping outside leaves you unable to
breathe and feeling like you were just beaten half to death
by a polar bear.

I was returning from a Bible study with several of my
friends. When we pulled into my driveway, I braced myself
for the cold and took a deep breath that I hoped would last
me until I got inside my house. Holding my breath, I jumped
out, waving good-bye to my homies, and dashed for the door.
I was about to open my door when all of a sudden it blasted
forward, almost knocking me over. A strong, invisible force
moved through my body pushing me backwards and causing me to exhale all the oxygen in my lungs. Someone or

something was coming out of the door as I was trying to go in. It was dark, so I couldn't make out who it was. Then a strange fear swept across my body emanating from my gut to the ends of my fingers. I had not felt this kind of fear since I was a kid and had to sleep alone in my room after seeing the movie *Nightmare on Elm Street*. I cannot begin to describe how frightened I was.

A few seconds went by and I gathered my wits and went inside. As I closed the door I slowly looked around the room without moving any farther into the darkness. Reaching for the light switch, I felt fear attacking me like a thug holding me hostage, demanding that I not turn the light on. I weighed the issue and thought it would be better to have the light on than to stand there freaking out in the dark. So I braved the vast unknown, determined to kill anything that might be hiding in the darkness. I flipped the switch and a sense of ease comforted my emotions as I welcomed the dim illumination the small lamp provided.

I went into my room, sat on my bed, and puzzled about what I was experiencing. I thought back to the conversations I'd had with my friends on the ride home. Were we talking about scary movies or childhood fears and now it was messing with my head? Flipping through the rewind feature in my mind, I dismissed that thought because we had spent almost all our time talking about feeding the poor and being Good Samaritans. With the shower scene from the movie *Psycho* playing in my head, I was feeling creeped out and decided to skip my evening shower. I pulled off my shoes and clothes and tried to snuggle under the covers.

As I lay there unable to sleep, I made another decision to keep my bedside lamp on. I kept rolling from one side to the other, glancing every now and then at the clock on the wall. Staring at the ticking timepiece, my heavy eyelids slowly closed across my field of vision as I noticed it was 1:00 a.m. before everything faded to black.

I welcomed the darkness of sleep. My nightly trips to dreamland always proved to be a great happy place for me. My dreams often helped me escape my prison of pain. Yet on this night my dreams took me behind cell bars—the type of iron bars that keep prisoners caged. It seemed so real that I reached out to grab one of the bars and discovered that it was scorching hot to the touch. I flinched back at the pain, and as I did, I bumped into someone who was standing behind me. I swiftly turned to see who it was, and when I saw the face, my knees buckled and I lost the ability to stand up.

Woozy and lightheaded, I tried to focus my eyes. I was now facedown on what appeared to be a black coal floor. My eyes quickly adjusted, and I could make out dirty feet protruding from under an even filthier white robe. I questioned what I thought I was seeing behind the robe. Were they the tips of extremely large feathers? As I looked up, I held my hands across my eyes and peered though the crack in my fingers. I wanted to know what it was, but I didn't dare look into those wild eyes again. It moved, and instantly a horrifying eye was staring back at me from the other side of my trembling hands.

The smell of sulfur and rotting garbage invaded my nose as the breath of the beast that stood before me spoke. Its voice did not fit its appearance as an alluring, enchanting female tone seductively said, "I have orders concerning you." I gagged on the vulgar stench seething from its mouth and desperately tried to breathe in some fresh air but failed to find any. As I turned my head away from its hypnotic gaze, my nose came in contact with the floor and the floor began to move. Suddenly a grimy, coal-covered hand grabbed my arm, followed by another and another. I was being pulled downward. I tried to push myself up but could not as hundreds of hands reaching up through the floor grasped my body. Instantly I found myself being tugged from behind, and after feeling a very brief tautness, I snapped upward and found myself floating above the reaching hands. What I saw next caused my stomach to knot up, and I projectile vomited.

What I thought was the floor was actually a pile of zombie-like, decaying bodies, writhing and scraping to be out from beneath the massive weight, desperately trying to breathe. But the place seemed to be void of air. Suspended in nothingness, I noticed two massive wings were flapping on both sides of me. But even they did not produce any wind. I started to become sick again because of the lack of oxygen mingled with the realization that I was being held by a fallen demonic angel over the vast ocean of bodies in the pit of hell.

The creature spoke again, but this time its voice sounded different. I was perplexed. *Is that a tone of thankfulness I'm picking up?* I asked myself. Yes it was, and it was clear and enchanting like the voice of a siren luring sailors to their death, all the while thanking them for taking to the sea. It grabbed my face with its hand and forced me to stare at the faces of the damned. Their eyes were filled with blood, and their thirsty tongues were wagging from their mouths as their outstretched hands reached for me.

Although they were not able to speak because the heat had completely dried out their vocal cords, my mind could some-how hear their thoughts, and I began hurting emotionally—nauseated with an overwhelming sense of personal responsibility for their plight. The fallen angel, almost in a melodious song, whispered through their screams, "Thank you for feeding their stomachs and leaving their souls alone."

As one of the outstretched hands grabbed me by my neck, I tried to scream, but not a sound came out of my mouth. I jerked awake staring at the ceiling in my small room. My whole body was paralyzed. I shifted my eyes as far as I could to the left and right, and the same sense of fear I had when I encountered that force earlier that night now had full domain over my entire mind and emotions. I was lying on a water-bed, sinking deep into it with the sides bulging with water. Something was on top of me, had me by my throat, and

124

was pressing me down into the bed. My heart raced wildly, sweat seeping from every pore of my body. I couldn't speak; I couldn't breathe. Fear was lording over me, so I began to pray. My lips made motions but my vocal cords were locked. I tried to say "Jesus, Jesus, Jesus!" My voice finally worked, and the air became filled with a loud screaming, "Jesus!" At the same moment, I sprang up in the bed as I was released from whatever it was that held me down.

I bobbed violently up and down for a moment as the weight was now off me and the waves in the waterbed slowly began to settle, causing the bobbing to subside. I sat there holding my heart. After one last little bob, I turned to the clock and it still read 1:00 a.m. No time had elapsed since I last looked at the clock. Crying, I called my mentor, Tommy Mallard, and asked him to pray over me. I am not sure what happened that night. It is still a mystery to me.

> *I operate from a deep conviction that everyone will spend forever somewhere, and I am certain there are only two final destinations: heaven and hell.*

Take a moment and exhale. That was quite a story wasn't it? To be completely honest, I'm not sure all of what I told you actually happened to me. Now don't write me hate mail and burn this book before you finish reading it. I wanted to start the chapter off by saying, "What you are about to read was based on a true story." Lots of elements really happened. I did get attacked by a demon one night. It did come out of my door as I was going in, and it did have me by my throat weighing me down in my waterbed. I couldn't speak, and I was paralyzed. It all happened at 1:00 a.m., and it was the most horrifying experience of my life.

But as for the details of the nightmare, they were thoughts that invaded my mind after I had the attack. The moment was as close to a surreal moment that I have experienced. Remember the thought I had about the possibility of Christians feeding a hungry man yet he dies and goes to hell on a full stomach because we only met his physical need and never dialed in on the condition of his soul? This trip to hell brings a sense of urgency to that concern.

Did I really experience the trip to hell? I'm kind of like Paul when he described his trip to heaven. He couldn't nail it down, so he said whether in the body or out of the body he did not know. But there is one thing that I am certain about. I operate from a deep conviction that everyone will spend forever somewhere, and I am certain there are only two final destinations: heaven and hell. A hurt healer's core mission is to make sure that hungry people get fed and that their thirsty souls get soaked with the refreshing waters of the gospel.

DELVE

What are your thoughts about encountering demons and spiritual warfare?

_____

_____

What description of hell did you find most horrifying in this story?

_____

_____

What emotions surged through your heart when you read that the demon thanked me for caring for the stomachs of people and leaving their souls alone?

_____

_____

_____

If it's true that everyone will spend forever somewhere, then what changes need to be made in your life to help others prepare for heaven?

God, if my spiritual eyes were opened, I would shudder at the thought of how many millions of demons I see waging war for the souls of my family and friends. Every human being will spend forever somewhere after death. Satan desires it to be hell, but your heart is for no one to perish. Help me catch your heart for the salvation of people's souls. Amen.

18

What Do I Do with That?

But when He saw the multitudes, He was moved with compassion for them, because they were weary and scattered.

Matthew 9:36

As a minister, I travel all across America, and I am frequently asked to counsel individuals who have been crushed by the fallout of our sin-cursed world. There are a great number of them in the world. My pastor, Dr. Johnny Hunt, often says about the people who come to our church, "On every pew is a broken heart." I would like to expand that statement a step further and say that behind every door to a home, college dorm, condo, or apartment is a broken heart. The people in the stories I'm about to share are real. Permission has been granted to share their stories, but their names have been changed to respect their privacy.

I have thousands of stories, but the one that came to mind first was a moment I had with a girl we will call Sarah. I was sitting at the end of a dock during a summer camp where I had been preaching three consecutive days and nights. I was thinking about when I could go home and get some real food when Sarah showed up. I'm guessing she was around sixteen years old. She was a short, petite girl, wearing a camp T-shirt and Bermuda shorts and sporting a brunette, spiked, punker hairdo. She didn't say anything to me for about thirty minutes, so I just sat there letting her be quiet as I enjoyed the silence. I had been counseling students all summer and was really hoping she would go away. I know you thought I was more spiritual than that, but I just didn't have it in me to try to emotionally deal with another painful adolescent story.

Sarah kept looking over at me from time to time, and her lips moved but she said nothing. Her eyes shifted nervously back and forth from me to the water. The intense sun was heating up my flip-flops and scorching my toes, so I thought it was a good time to go inside. I stood up and started to leave when she spoke. Her head was bowed toward the water, and her bangs cascaded over the sides of her face. Hidden in her slouch and hair she muttered, "How did you do it?" Her voice was shaky, but the tone was authentically inquisitive.

"Do what?" I replied.

Her head still down, she began to sway her legs back and forth, her toes skimming the surface of the water. She replied, "Get over your pain." She had heard me share my testimony earlier that morning.

"Who said I was over it?" She turned and faced me full on. Her eyes seemed to question my response, and if I could have read her mind, I'm sure she was thinking, *You're not over it either?* But she didn't say a word. She just sat there and let the tears flow. It was awkward to observe. Her lips didn't quiver, nor was there any sniffling of the nose. Her huge, brilliant blue eyes never blinked as tears streamed down her cheeks, leaving dark blue spots on her light blue shirt. Then she dumped the bomb on me: "My mother has been pimping me to the guys in our neighborhood to support her drug habit since I was thirteen years old." My heart sank, and I was arrested with the thought, *What do you do with that, Tony? How in the world do you engage that kind of pain?*

Next story—a scary night with my friend Jason. The backyard of the house I grew up in served as a neighborhood bar of sorts. Nobody ever asked for permission to be on our property, nor did my parents ever seem to mind. At the end of just about every day, once the sun set many of my neighbors would come over and converge around a bonfire with their beer and drugs. Before my conversion I spent a lot of time hanging out around that fire getting buzzed and listening to the guys tell tall tales and crude jokes. You remember my neighborhood, right? Then you'll understand when I tell you that the guys around the fire were like modern-day pirates of the Caribbean. They were rough individuals—the kind of guys Jesus would hang out with and try to love into his family. So after my conversion, I often found myself back out there letting God love them through me.

How in the world do you engage that kind of pain?

I recall a very scary and sad moment one cold night in late February—the kind of evening where you can see the steam from your breath. It was 11:00 p.m., and I decided to stroll into my backyard and mingle with my old buddies. Jason was the only one out that night. Perfect! I had been sharing the gospel with Jason and had been waiting for the perfect opportunity to invite him to respond to Jesus's invitation to be forgiven and free.

Jason was the poster child of all my pirate friends. We even called him "Pirate." He looked like he had just walked off the set with Captain Jack Sparrow. When he laughed, his smile showed off black, empty spaces where teeth once were. He had a scar across his face tracing the diagonal path an assailant's blade had taken across his right eye, through the middle of his nose, and down his left cheek. His right arm proudly displayed a vibrant, colorful tattoo, but its image and message were gruesomely dark. At first glance it looked like a classic skull and crossbones. But if you looked a little closer you could see that double-barrel shotguns were actually in the place where the bones normally were. The skull had a sinister smile—an attitude supporting the motto below the guns: "Once is not enough." If you know anything about the tattoo culture, then you know that behind most tattoos is a story—usually one about someone they loved who passed away, such as a baby, brother, or parent.

Jason's was also about someone who died—someone who died by his hand! Back before I met him, Jason had blown away a man in Texas with a double-barrel shotgun. He was paid to do it by the Mexican drug cartel. They told him he would go to prison but that their lawyers would get him out on self-defense in five years. Like I said, Jason was a pirate!

Jason knew how to get a good fire going. Dry tree limbs were crackling and emitting small bits of sparking embers onto the dirt. Pushed by the brisk, icy night air on my back and lured by the warmth, I pressed in close and snuggled my face and hands. Looking into the blazing tree limbs, I couldn't see Jason. I knew he was on the other side of the fire, so I got right to the point. "Jason, you've seen how Jesus has changed my life in the past few weeks, and I'm telling you, bro, that he can change yours as well. I've told you what the Bible says you need to do to receive Jesus's forgiveness. Jason, would you like to experience that tonight?"

Jason's response was quick and definitive: "I can't!"

I was struck by his reply. Not by what he said but by the tone in which he said it. His voice was desperate. It wasn't that he didn't want to; he was saying that he couldn't do it. "What makes you think you can't?" I shot back.

"Tony, I know that the good side is real. Not just 'cuz you have changed so much but because I've seen the bad side—the evil side." He gripped a beer can in one hand, and with the other hand he held the rest of the six-pack. He was clearly falling apart. The bronze reflection of the flames intermingled with flickering shadows that licked across his grief-stricken face. He pulled the can up to his mouth and chugged the remaining contents of the can and tossed it into the fire. A metal tinkling sound accompanied by a small hiss of steam from the evaporating backwash filled the air, followed by a very long moment of silence. He just sat there with a look of horror in his eyes.

As Jason kept looking into the fire, he spoke again—this time with the voice of a scared child who wanted desperately to be told everything was going to be okay. "When the lawyers didn't show up in five years to get me out of prison, I got scared. I couldn't live and die in prison. So I made a deal with the devil." Jason looked up at me with a tear in his eye. His bottom lip quivered, and he popped open another beer. "Satan was in our prison, Tony, and he made me an offer: he would give me my freedom in exchange for my soul. I took him up on it. I can never be forgiven; I already gave up my soul." His hand was shaking as he pressed the beer can up to his lips and muttered, "I'm damned; I'm damned," before he kicked his head back and drained the entire can.

As I watched him guzzle that alcohol, I found myself struggling with a reply and haunted by that blasted question, *What do I do with that?*

I wish my head had a USB port on its side like my computer does. If it did, I would invite you to plug in and have access to the full memories I have of those two stories and countless others that I have experienced over the last seventeen years of being in ministry. I'd love for you to experience what I saw, heard, and felt. Like the executive I met on a plane who was suicidal over his pending divorce, which was brought on by his inescapable addiction to frequenting sex clubs. Or the time I visited a ranch for girls with eating disorders who were on the verge of starving themselves to death because the mirror didn't tell them they were as beautiful as I saw them to be. Or the hundreds of times I have held the hands of hurting people who were fighting to hold onto hope as their loved ones were dying. In each of those cases I found myself haunted with the question, *What do I do with that?*

132

Even as I'm writing this, I'm thinking about you. I don't know you, but I'm sure you know people who have suffered from the sin and pain that this cursed world can dish out. You work with them; you live next door to them; you buy your coffee from them. They are bent out of shape because they were ambushed by the thief Satan and are spiritually and emotionally bleeding from divorce, a layoff at work, drug addiction, porn, alcohol abuse, or a previous painful mistake; or they were a victim of someone's pride or lust. And as I mentioned earlier, maybe you have gone through one or more of these painful experiences. If so, then I know you understand why I feel so strongly about making sure something is done to help others. But what can be done?

Has the same question that haunts me—*What do I do with that?*—ever caused you deep restlessness as well? The answers many Christians give to this question just pour fuel on the distressful fire already raging in hurting people's lives. I will explain this in depth in the next chapter.

D E L V E

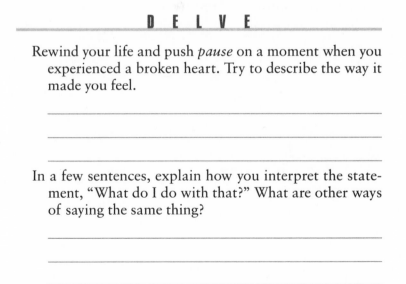

Rewind your life and push *pause* on a moment when you experienced a broken heart. Try to describe the way it made you feel.

_____

_____

_____

In a few sentences, explain how you interpret the statement, "What do I do with that?" What are other ways of saying the same thing?

_____

_____

_____

What current situation is someone you know personally going through that has caused you to ask that same question?

_____

_____

_____

In what ways do you find yourself responding to the needs of others?

_____

_____

_____

O Holy Spirit, breathe on me and grant me your sweet, caring interest for the needs of others. As I continue through the next few chapters, help me to hear your answer to the question, "What do I do with that?" Amen.

19

Step Over

And let us not grow weary while doing good, for in due season
we shall reap if we do not lose heart.

Galatians 6:9

Busy.

Slow down and let's say that word one more time.

Busy.

In our fast-paced, digital, millennium generation, we know
all about *busy*. We work ridiculous hours, get involved in
more activities than we can even attend, all the while taking
on bigger projects, trying to get ahead, or making sure we
leverage our upside. We know *busy*, but it isn't something
new. It's been around a while. I can trace it back at least two
thousand years.

Remember the swirling dust devils that were licking the
ground on which the hurting man lay bleeding to death in the
story of the Good Samaritan? Let's take a little trip together
back to that place in time.

The priest was the first person to come upon the victim. Do you remember his response? Yeah you do, because we tend to remember the bad things people do more easily than the good things. Keep that in mind as you live in a world of hurting people who need you and the gospel you live. The priest walked right past the hurting man.

I am a visual story guy, so when I read a story I often hear stories inside the stories. They are not new interpretations of the Scriptures. Rather they are just thoughts I have that help me grasp the moment and make it less academic and more human. Like you probably do, I had several thoughts about why a priest, a God-fearing humanitarian, would walk right past someone in need. I discussed many of these thoughts earlier, but another idea I considered is that he might have been in a hurry to get somewhere. I say this because I have been there many times myself. Have you? Sure you have. So it was easy for me to imagine how that moment could have played out from the priest's point of view.

> The priest wakes up that morning and takes a look at his to-do list for the day. It is filled with the things he was supposed to have done yesterday and many more things he should have accomplished weeks ago. He determines that today will be different.

Ever been there? He needs to have meetings with several people in Jericho, and nothing is going to get in the way of making those meetings happen—including the guy who is lying in the road the priest has to travel to get to those meetings.

> When he first sees the guy, he starts doing the math. Five minutes to resuscitate him; thirty minutes to clean up the

wounds. Add one extra hour to the trip because he will have to carry him and make frequent stops to rest; another thirty minutes to find an inn that will take him; forty-five more minutes to get him settled into his room and acclimated to his surroundings; twenty minutes to brief the innkeeper on the situation; then twenty-five minutes to take a different route within the city to get to his first meeting; and finally, twenty more minutes explaining to them why he was late. That adds up to almost four hours!

As the priest computes the numbers, he walks by the guy and sees that the disfigured man has his hand outstretched toward him. But the priest keeps his eyes straight ahead and his face toward his scheduled appointments. The dust on the road stirs up under his feet as he picks up the corners of his priestly robe and his pace to compensate for all the time lost thinking about the situation.

I really think that the priest's increased speed was probably more related to everyday math that says the farther you get away from the sound of someone's voice screaming, "Please help me!" the better your chances of not having to hear it. Either way, Jesus says that he passed the guy by.

I know what you are thinking here—that my version of the story is merely conjecture—and I have already admitted that it is. I just know that the guy in ministry over two thousand years ago did not help. I also know that there are still people in ministry today who fail to help, and a lot of that failure is due to being busy. People everywhere are in a hurry. We have things to do and places to be. So we avoid anything that might come up to sidetrack us from the journey toward our scheduled appointment.

In his book *Tipping Point: How Little Things Can Make a Big Difference*, Malcolm Gladwell has an interesting insight on the power of context. He refers to an experiment conducted by John Darley and Daniel Batson, two Princeton

University psychologists. They asked a group of students from Princeton Theological Seminary to prepare a short, extemporaneous talk on the biblical theme of the Good Samaritan. The students were assigned the task in one building but were told to go to another nearby building to give the talk. Along the way, each student ran into a man slumped in an alley, head down, eyes closed, coughing and groaning. The experiment was to see who would stop and help.

A lot of our failure to help is due to being busy.

Before the task was given, each student was also asked to fill out a questionnaire that gave evidence that each person was in ministry to help people. Once given the assignment, half the students were told they had plenty of time to get to the room and give their talk, and the rest were told that they were late and should hurry. The study revealed that out of the group that was told they had plenty of time, 63 percent stopped to help. Out of the group that was told they were in a rush, only 10 percent stopped to help the man in need. Malcolm says this study reveals that the words "you're late" had the effect of turning a person who was ordinarily compassionate into someone who was indifferent to suffering. This is not conjecture but a real case study that shows that when people are in a hurry, even those with high regard for helping others seldom stop to help a person who is hurting.

Remember that one of the reasons I am writing this book is for them—the people who get passed by. They need a voice, and I am willing to be that voice even if it means I get misunderstood and ostracized. One of the reasons I will take such a risk has to do with my biological mom. Earlier I told you that my mother was a very immoral, mentally unstable woman who worked the streets in Jacksonville, Florida, to survive.

I've taken many trips to Eighth Street. I recall driving those streets and having my heart break at the sight and smell of the landscape of the hopeless. The sounds of gunshots, police sirens, barking stray dogs, and a young gangster kid asking me if I want to buy some crack whirled around in my head, and I imagined what a cold, scary life of unpredictable pain my mom endured.

I remember waving off the gangsta thug wannabe, letting him know I had zero interest in his business endeavors, when I noticed an old, large church across the street. It was weathered and in need of a makeover, but it must have been something glorious back in the day. Its limestone steeple stretched toward heaven, held up by a genius, gothic architectural design complete with gargoyles and stained glass windows whose images told the story of Jesus.

Out front on the unlevel, crabgrass-infested sidewalk was a bench at a city bus stop. Someone was lying across it under some newspaper. People walked by, and some who were dressed for work seemed to not even notice the person was there. But they had to know someone was there because otherwise they would be sitting on that bench instead of standing next to it looking straight ahead as if the bench was there just to stand near. My mind flashed back in time, and I imagined that very scene being a picture of one of the many sad moments of my mother's life. My heart sank, and began to grieve deeply as I contemplated how many times my mother might have been passed out on that very bench years ago after going through a horrendous night of sexual favors in exchange for a few Abraham Lincolns.

I wondered how many churchgoing people walked right by her or around her with their eyes straight ahead, hurrying off to Sunday school or the eleven o'clock worship service. Then to top off their oblivious cruelty, once the service was over they walked right past her again in a hurry to get to a nearby restaurant to avoid the crowds and a long wait. My heart is pained even now as I think about it.

A couple of years ago I was at the Casting Crowns video shoot of their song, "Does Anybody Hear Her?" for the

Lifesong Live DVD. It was shot on the grand and picturesque campus of Berry College. If you have never seen that video, I encourage you to get the DVD and listen to the song and then watch the backstage action in the bonus material.

There is also a behind-the-scenes feature that shows us having a blast during that shoot. I spoof lead vocalist Mark Hall in one of the interviews as the camera crew shoots a scene that doesn't have Mark in it. I commented that because of Mark's absence it will be the best part of the whole video. There is another clip where the band is watching former drummer Andy Williams go crazy on a sugar rush, and Mark says they have special security agents positioned on the church roof with blow darts filled with Ritalin in case they have to use it on Andy. The laughter was much needed and welcomed because the subject of the song is so intense.

The song is about a girl who is sinking in hurt and sin and needs what Christians have. But she can't seem to get it because we Christians live our lives without any notice of her pain or presence.

The sun was beginning to set, casting a long shadow of the Gothic features of the campus chapel. The dark outline of an ornate cross stretching out from the peak of the roof gave me a haunting flashback of the park bench in my mother's neighborhood. My heart sank thinking about her living in the shadow of a church's steeple as the members of that church walked right by, seemingly unaware of her presence. She lay undetected, like a shipwrecked sailor perishing on a deserted island as airplanes loaded with life-sustaining cargo fly overhead. Just like the Casting Crowns song says, we have the hope, joy, and peace that this world needs, but in our busyness we pass right by the people who desperately need it. It's no wonder those stranded people have a poor impression of Jesus. Too often those who follow Christ claim to have a corner on the market of eternity but live like they don't have enough time in the day to help others prepare for it. Ouch!

D E L V E

Close your eyes and think about the busy people in your life. What are they busy doing?

_____

_____

_____

What are you busy doing?

_____

_____

_____

Describe how you felt when you heard Jesus say that the priest passed by the Hurting Heart guy.

_____

_____

_____

Write down the feelings and thoughts that come to your mind regarding the idea of giving away what we have "tucked away."

_____

_____

_____

_Dear Lord Jesus, I confess my own propensity to
be preoccupied with the short-lived, insignificant
pursuit of the urgent. Today I choose to unplug from
my busy matrix and slow down enough to give away
what I have tucked away. Amen._

20

Pass On

Whoever shuts his ears to the cry of the poor will also cry
himself and not be heard.

Proverbs 21:13

When our personal comfort zone clashes with someone else's
personal hell on earth, we are prone to get overwhelmed and
ask, "What do I do with that?" In the last chapter we looked
at one of the responses we tend to have toward others as seen
in the life of the priest. But if you lean into Jesus's story a
bit further, you will discover a similar, yet distinctly different course of action, or lack thereof, taken by the Levite.
Let's throw some binoculars on the Levite's life for a few
minutes.

I envision the Levite caught up in the hustle and bustle of
the town crowd that morning. He starts his day getting something hot to drink to take the edge off the morning dew that's
icing up his already cold bones. Days can be terribly hot in

the Middle East and the nights arctic cold if you are anything like my wife, who thinks it's freezing at 75 degrees.

The market is alive with the noise of clucking chickens and rattling vending carts along with the shouts of merchants inviting shoppers to consider their goods. *So much for a quiet morning*, thinks the Levite as he munches down a small, cooked egg. Just then several of the city's businessmen come along and he tosses them a heartfelt "good morning." They return a courtesy "good morning" back at him.

Small talk quickly turns into big business as the men begin to discuss all the money being made in Jericho. Before long about twenty of them are shaking hands and confirming plans to meet up later that day and make the trip down to Jericho together. The idea of having company on his trip reveals the Levite's anxiety about traveling alone because outlaws are known to wait in ambush on that stretch of road. But he can't wait till noon; he has plans that require him to be in Jericho early. So he decides to head on and settles with knowing the businessmen will not be far behind him. He purchases a few figs along with some small slices of bread, fills his wineskin, and off he goes.

The Levite is well over halfway to Jericho. The hot sun is making every step a welcomed one, knowing it is taking him closer to some long-awaited shade. He can hear the slow clack of donkey hooves trailing not too far behind him—it's the businessmen. Comforted with the knowledge that they are only about a mile back, he feels safe enough to take his eyes off the road and enjoy a little snack.

He loves figs and has been waiting to eat the ones he bought in the market since ten minutes into his trip. He bites into the fig and swallows the sweet, gritty fruit with a chaser of wine, but he just about chokes on it when he looks up and sees a bloody body at the side of the road! Suddenly the body moves, and he's so startled that the remaining wine

> sprays out of his mouth. He slowly approaches the groaning
> person. He comes right up and stands over the victim and
> stares at him for a long while. Perhaps he wants to find out if
> it's someone he knows. Or maybe he's like most Americans;
> when we see a terrible wreck on the highway, we stretch our
> necks to catch a glimpse of the carnage as we slowly drive by.
> When the victim squirms again, the Levite darts off.

I want to interrupt this story right here and say that when I read in the Bible that this guy "came and looked, and passed by on the other side" (Luke 10:32), I freaked! Have you ever lost your breath because your heart dropped into your feet at the sight of injustice? I was there! I have this 3-D picture of the moment in my head. I see the Levite walking toward me in my mind's eye. I see the victim lying on the ground behind him, barely able to look up and slumping down as he watches the Levite walk away. My mind starts going into overdrive, and I find myself chasing down the Levite on that road to ask him a few questions.

> **Me:** Hey bro, what's up with the "leave the hurting guy in the street" thing going on here?
>
> **Levite:** Oh, well, um, I . . . I . . . I don't do the blood thing very well.
>
> **Me:** Nobody does the blood thing very well, dude. Let's go back there and help that guy.
>
> **Levite:** Me? Oh no, I wouldn't even know where to start to help him.
>
> **Me:** How about we start with letting him have the rest of that wine in your wineskin and that last fig in your pocket?
>
> **Levite:** No, no, it's . . . it's not enough. And besides, right behind me is a large group of businessmen, and I'm sure they will be able to help him.

I stop trailing the Levite and watch him walk off into the distance, finally disappearing over the hill. And in my heart and gut there is a weighty and dull void of anything worth

144   **SHOWING JESUS**

ever feeling again, and I hear the whisper in my ear, "Tony, do you feel that? This is how our encounters with Christianity have left us feeling, and it's why we say Christianity sucks." It's their voices. "We are that guy in the road, and we are emotionally and spiritually bleeding to death while most Christians pass by our hurts thinking someone else is going to tend to us."

You may need to pause and take a deep breath after that statement. I did. But please don't dismiss my version of the story as mere conjecture. Will you try to go there with me? This make-believe scenario might be a whole lot more real than we care to admit. I'm claiming that the Levite said there were other people out there who would help that hurting man. He was confident that someone else would come along to do what he knew should be done but he wouldn't do. I know that we don't know for sure that this happened. It may just be a crazy moment of my wild imagination. But this kind of thing really happens all the time in our own backyard in America.

> *The Levite was confident that someone else would come along to do what he knew should be done but he wouldn't do.*

In my Cultural Milieu class at the Criswell Center for Biblical Studies, I heard a story about a crime that rocked America. On March 13, 1964, a twenty-four-year-old woman by the name of Kitty Genovese was murdered in Queens, New York, by Winston Moseley. Moseley stabbed her and raped her in an alley for thirty-five minutes until she died. You may be wondering how that could rock America since people get killed in worse situations than that in New York all the time. Well, what was different about this killing is that it occurred while thirty-eight of her neighbors heard the attack happen from their windows and did nothing about it. The case caused a national uproar with people wailing about the dehumanization of urban America. The event even landed a name as a new sociological disorder called the "Genovese syndrome."

There are many experts who have weighed in on what caused the people to just stand by and do nothing to help. I am not sure why they didn't help, but looking back, I can adamantly say that it was *wrong*! Remember my saying, "To not help is to hurt"? I still believe it. And in the case of Kitty Genovese, it proved to be right. The murderer actually stabbed Kitty and then left the scene. The police investigation revealed that thirty-eight neighbors heard her scream during the first attack. Then after a few minutes he came back and repeatedly stabbed her again as she screamed for help. Some of the neighbors glanced out of their windows. The attacker took another break. She yelled and yelled for help, which she did not get. In some stories I have heard others tell about the event, someone said that one man actually turned up his radio to drown out her screaming. How sad is that? Moseley resumed his attack and proceeded to rape and cut her until she bled to death. No one did anything during that thirty-five-minute period of time. Finally, after the attack was over, one elderly man called the police.

I propose to you that there were thirty-nine crimes committed that night: one by Winston Moseley and one by each of the thirty-eight people who stood by doing nothing to prevent it. Our professor, Dr. Kirk Spencer, told us that when the police asked the neighbors why they did nothing, one man replied that he didn't want to get involved, and most of them said they thought someone else would help.

Winston Moseley is seventy-two years old at the time I am writing this book, and he is shut up in jail for life. There is another murderer named Satan, however, who is roaming about "like a roaring lion, seeking whom he may devour" (1 Peter 5:8). It does not take long to realize he is having his fill of stealing, killing, and destroying human lives. Like Moseley, his attacks are relentless. The knives he uses to deliver the wounds are divorce, porn addiction, social injustice, poverty, drug addiction, racism, and anything else he can use to stab us deeply and hurt us indefinitely.

Have you heard the cries of your neighbors, classmates, coworkers, and family members? Think about it. I'm sure you know someone right now who is crushed by a large burden and needs your help. What has been your response to that person's pain? Perhaps you simply said what I have said so many times myself: "What do I do with that?" I understand the question, but let me beg you to make sure that you avoid the mistake the Levite made by thinking someone else will come behind you and take care of

> *The knives Satan uses are divorce, porn addiction, social injustice, poverty, drug addiction, racism, and anything else he can use to stab us deeply and hurt us indefinitely.*

something that needs your attention now. The person in pain is asking, "Will you be a hurt ignorer or a hurt healer?"

DELVE

The Levite thought that the businessmen behind him would help the victim. What feedback would you give him about that?

_____

_____

_____

Have you ever not helped someone because you thought someone else would? What thoughts or explanations did you use at the time?

_____

_____

_____

Try to rapidly write down each emotion you felt as you read the Kitty Genovese story. Once you have written them down, review them. Don't ever forget the way the story made you feel, and let it inspire you to be a hurt healer.

_____

_____

_____

What answer would you give a hurting person who asks, "Will you be a hurt healer or a hurt ignorer?"

_____

_____

_____

God, as I peer out of the window of my everyday life, I am aware that many around me are under attack by a robber more sinister than Winston Moseley. I commit to not be like those window gazers who stood by and did nothing for Kitty. I must assume no one else will help, and therefore I must take action to become a lifeline for you to use to rescue those who are in need. Amen.

21

Pass Out

I can do all things through Christ who strengthens me.

Philippians 4:13

The job of a hurt healer is exhausting work. Caring for the hurting can take its toll on you emotionally, physically, and spiritually. Putting it frankly, it's bloody warfare!

Did you see the movie *Saving Private Ryan*, directed by Steven Spielberg? I am intrigued by the bravery of men in combat, so I decided to see the movie. In short, the motion picture is about Captain John Miller, who leads a unit of Army Rangers that storm the beaches of Normandy and later are given the assignment of securing Army Private James Francis Ryan of the 101 Airborne Division and sending him back home to the States. It is a visual masterpiece with an inspiring storyline.

As I watch that kind of movie, I find myself asking how I would respond if I were in their shoes. In all honesty, my answer is not as courageous as the conduct of the American soldiers in Spielberg's film. There is one scene, however, that I felt I could identify with and so could every other person who has attempted to be a hurt healer.

It's 6:30 a.m. on June 6, 1944, and a group of soldiers who survived the nightmarish landing are now storming up the green section of Omaha Beach. The Germans, nesting on top of the beach's ridge, are picking them off by the thousands with every kind of artillery power conceivable—rifles, machine guns, and mortars. Death is having an orgy on that beach. The air is filled with shouts of captains and sergeants giving orders and wounded soldiers shouting, "Medic!" Ammo, cover, and medics are in high demand that day, and all are in short supply. In this scene, a medic is kneeling on the beach working frantically on several soldiers at one time as mortar shells explode and bullets make eruptions in the sand all around him. One young soldier, who looks about eighteen years old, was hit pretty hard, but the medic's evaluation indicates that he will survive with treatment. The other men around him are already dead.

The young boy pitifully cries out to the medic and says he just wants to go home. The medic's heart is touched by his plea, and with a tender smile he tells the boy he will make it. At that very moment the enemy fires again and kills the boy.

It is a grotesque visual depiction of the hell those soldiers underwent. What the medic did next opened up my tear ducts, and my already broken heart gushed out its sympathy. The medic quickly turns his attention to the boy to whom he had just given hope. The bullets continue to rip into the boy and the other soldiers' bodies that are surrounding the medic. In an act of frustration and anger intermingled with horror, the medic beats his fists on the chest of that boy while looking up at the Germans' nest and screaming at the top of his lungs, "Give us a break! Give us a break! Give us a break!"

I was not among those who stormed the beaches of Normandy. My respect for them is profound, and they have no equals in the Hall of Honor. I am an optimistic person, and

I'm positive about today and my future. But I am also a realist, and when I look at the human experience, it resembles one big D-day. Satan relentlessly and viciously bombards us with his fiery darts from his perch as the prince and power of the air. The carnage of mangled marriages, decomposing dreams, and hemorrhaging hearts are piled high, stinking up what would otherwise be a beautiful beach.

As a hurt healer, I can identify with that medic. I have heard my name called many times by those who have taken a hit from the enemy: the weeping parents who are struggling with two jobs and trying to care for their nine-year-old quadriplegic who is confined to a wheelchair and fed through a tube; the unemployed dad who listens to his boy cry himself to sleep because he hasn't eaten in three days; the sick girl who can't stop bleeding from the self-induced abortion she administered in an alleyway; the orphaned children whose parents were slaughtered because of their ethnicity; the Sarahs who have been pimped and the Jasons who have committed dreadful sins the devil won't let them forget about. I have found myself many times beating my fist on the floor of my prayer closet exhausted, frustrated, on the verge of passing out, begging an unseen enemy to give me a break.

I recall one moment like that in my prayer time when I was totally spent and on the verge of disengaging altogether. It revolved around a poverty-stricken person who had been sexually abused. Those stories always hit a little too close to home for me. The person had so many questions, and the abuse kept coming. Eventually the person committed suicide. I was in my prayer closet and it was as if I was beating that person's chest trying to resuscitate him as I was screaming out loud for our enemy Satan to back off. I was crying out for a break!

And God did what only he can do. He spoke and gave me hope and a broader perspective. He said, "Tony, when did the break come for those men storming that beach?"

In my thoughts I said, "Only after they took out every one of those gun nests." It's a funny thing how God can hear us even when we don't speak a word.

He replied, "A break is coming for you and all of humanity. One day I will take Satan out finally and forever by casting him into the burning lake of fire."

I immediately shot back in anger, "Well, that may take another thousand years. Until then, what do I do? I don't have what it takes to take care of all of these wounded, hurting people."

What God said next has empowered me throughout my years of ministry. He calmly encouraged me and said, "Yes you do, son. You have the same thing the Good Samaritan had, and that's oil and wine."

By now you should know that I can be a little on the spiritually goofy side at times. So I blurted out, "So what do you want me to do? Help them get drunk and get a tan?"

I pictured God smiling at my antics, and then he explained. "You have the wine of my forgiveness and the oil of my love, and that will be enough." God's forgiveness and love are two powerful resources that remedy serious hurts that are a result of this intense, exhausting battle.

If you become a hurt healer, it will bring you personal hurt that will need to be healed itself because it requires so much of your time, money, and heart. As I look around at the landscape of Christianity, this is probably one of the biggest reasons so many Christians are not engaged. But the good news is, we don't have to go it alone, and we have all the resources available to do it in God's power.

I have often told the story about a little boy who wanted to do something special for his dad. This eleven-year-old boy decided to mow the front lawn for his dad. He worked on it for about an hour, and it was looking really good. The lawn had perfect symmetrical lines from the mower running across it, and the hedges were precisely manicured. There was only one eyesore. His dad had placed some large boulders throughout the yard as lawn décor. (This, I hasten to add, is something we dads need to stop doing—garnishing our dwellings with hideous lawn décor. Leave it to the ladies, guys.)

The rocks had high blades of grass protruding up along the edges because the boy didn't have a Weed Eater. So the boy came up with an idea to make them look better—he would pluck each blade out by hand. After an hour and still having several boulders to do, he knew he had to come up with a better plan or else he would be a senior in college by the time he finished.

His next idea was genius. He thought if he simply moved the rocks, he could take the mower and mow over the circle of high grass and then put the rock back into its place, leaving the area clean-cut like the rest of the yard. So he put both hands on the first rock and began to push. He pushed hard, but it would not move. He leaned over into it and shoved with all the strength his arms and legs could gather. It still did not move.

As the boy was frantically pushing, his dad pulled into the driveway and noticed his son grunting, with his head bobbing up and down, trying to move the rock. The dad thought, *Awesome, this is going to be some great entertainment.* He got out of the car and leaned against the fence watching, completely undetected by his son. After a few moments of more head bobbing and grunting, the boy collapsed over the boulder. As he lay there sweating profusely, his father spoke up. "Son, did you try with everything you've got to move that rock?"

The boy's expression said, "Dad, you must have an IQ equivalent to this rock. How long have you been watching me?" But he replied, "Yes, I tried with everything I've got."

To which the dad replied, "No you haven't, son. Because you have failed to ask your father to move it for you."

Humanity's problem is not that we have fathers who put large rocks in our lawns. But we all have heavy "issue" boulders in the lawn of our hearts, and we exhaust ourselves trying to clean up around them. The good news of the gospel is that God, like a caring Father, is leaning against the fence of eternity ready to move them for us. And this refreshing victory happens as needy, hurting people experience the wine of his forgiveness and the oil of his love.

D E L V E

Reflect for a moment on D-day as a metaphor for the Christian life. In what way do you agree or disagree with that idea?

_____

_____

_____

What are your own personal limitations that cause you to get overwhelmed?

_____

_____

_____

How does it make you feel to know that we have everything we need through God's power to help those in need?

_____

_____

_____

God, how many times have I found myself overwhelmed by the vast needs of those around me? In my weakness, I have almost given up. Thank you today for the reminder that through your power, I have all I need to be able to help effectively. Amen.

22

Wine of Forgiveness

Then Jesus said, "Father, forgive them."

Luke 23:34

My father-in-law may be a tough fighter pilot, but I'm going to let you in on a little secret. He passes out at the sight of blood. It's really kind of funny. (It won't be funny when he reads this because he will come looking for some of mine.) I know very few people who don't get anxious when they see blood. When Jesus told the crowd that the Samaritan bandaged the victim's wounds, I imagine faces grimaced and eyes squinted at the thought of what that actually looked and felt like for the victim. I'm grimacing now, and I'm sure the Samaritan did his share of it since he actually saw the wounds.

> Once the Samaritan dismounts his animal, he does a quick examination to determine the necessary treatment. The victim's arm is bent outward between his elbow and wrist.

155

Wow, that's a nasty break, he thinks. The man's left leg is swollen three times its normal size between the knee and the ankle. "Another break," he says under his breath. Both eyes are black-and-blue, and his nose is seeping blood. His off-white cloak has a massive red blood stain on it, which is checkered with several small incisions that hint toward stab wounds. Tearing open the clothing leaves no doubt. The thieves were vicious, and the poor man has more than ten large wounds to his stomach and chest. The small slits along his arms and hands explain why the injuries aren't any worse—this guy fought for his life, and the Samaritan isn't going to let him lose it.

He makes splints for the broken bones from tree branches. Then to mend the cuts, he uses oil, wine, and a few strips of cloth torn from his robe. First he has to apply the wine to clean out the wound. Thieves are known to carry two knives: one they keep clean for personal use, and the other is never cleaned, which allows for germs to populate, thus making the strike more severe. (I guess our modern-day tyrants were not the ones who invented biological warfare after all.)

The openings are already beginning to swell, causing the flesh at the point of each incision to protrude outward, making the wound stay open and susceptible to dirt and debris. The alcohol in the wine provides an antiseptic to combat infection. The cuts are nasty and dirty, so the Samaritan keeps pouring on the wine and holding the man's hands back as his spontaneous reflexes cause him to try to grab the place from which the pain emanates. As the wine penetrates through the blood clots and mud, the victim lets out several deep, loud, vocal-cord-shredding screams. It is painful but necessary.

That's the way it goes with God's forgiveness. To be forgiven means we are guilty of doing something wrong. To receive forgiveness, we must admit the fault. Before we can

SHOWING JESUS

do that, we have to recount and remember what we did. With that comes the pain. For forgiveness to penetrate and soothe those hurts, wounds are torn open and the pain intensifies. But once it gets through the surface, forgiveness does its antiseptic magic. It cleanses the infectious wounds sin created and enables you to move on to a better quality of life.

> *For forgiveness to penetrate and soothe those hurts, wounds are torn open and the pain intensifies.*

People need to know God forgives them. But that requires admission of guilt. It's a painful part of the process of recovery, but the outcome is oh so sweet. What a joy for sinners to admit their sins, be forgiven by God, have their guilt burden lifted, and ultimately gain access into heaven where they will live forever in celebration with throngs of the forgiven.

As I have been telling you, being a hurt healer is bloody warfare, which is why many Christians hold back forgiveness. Even though they enjoy the benefits of being forgiven from God, most Christians are not willing to forgive others. We hold the unchurched hostage with our gun of holiness, demanding that they live up to a standard that is impossible to reach because they are dead in their sins. As I look around me, I am crushed by the bitterness I see in the hearts of Christians toward abortion doctors, homosexuals, thieves, murderers, liars, druggies, whores, politicians, business competitors, other denominations, and the lists goes on and on.

Someone once told me that bitterness does more damage to the person who has stored it up than to the people upon whom it is poured. When that person shared this insight about bitterness, I happened to be really upset with some people in the church who were mad at me over some students who were smoking on the church campus. The kids were skaters who hung outside doing tricks in the parking lot before they came in to check out the music and critique the message. Our ministry provided trash cans filled with sand to be used as ash trays for them. Some people told me I was condoning their conduct, but I said Jesus has to change their hearts before he can change their habits. It was war, and I was hot! I wish I could take it back now, but I looked at the bitterness expert and said, "Then I won't have any trouble because I'm not storing up any bitterness; I'm pouring it all out on them!"

The truth is, I had become bitter at people who were bitter toward sinners, and it ended up hurting me and the ministry we were attempting. So I understand bitterness and how it can destroy you. It is so much better to just forgive because I have learned the valuable lesson about how forgiveness blesses both the forgiver and the forgiven.

> **Even though they enjoy the benefits of being forgiven from God, most Christians are not willing to forgive others.**

I have many stories about forgiveness that I would love to share. Most of them are full of sadness and tears, like when I met and forgave the man who physically and sexually abused me for the first three years of my life. That's a heavy tearjerker for sure. But so much of this book has been on the serious, dark side that I've got to laugh a little or I'm gonna go nuts. So let me tell you a humorous story and hopefully swing back around and make a serious point about forgiveness.

One night while I was driving home, some boys hiding in the woods threw eggs at my van. I was determined to catch the culprits. We had just gotten ice cream, and my children were eating in their seats when it happened. At the sound of the eggs crashing on the side of the van, I mashed down the gas pedal and turned into the park like a wild man. My kids were slung across the van from the g-force. With their ice cream and faces smashed against the windows, they were screaming, "Daddy, have you lost your mind?" What I did next kind of indicates they may have been right.

I screeched up to a small line of pine trees that I figured the eggers were hiding in. I jumped out of the van and raced to the edge of the small forest screaming, "Come out, boys;

I know you're in there!" Nothing happened. Then I heard some laughter and saw the brush move. I raced toward the movement, and as I did, I tripped over a motorized scooter one of the vandals had left behind.

I took the scooter to my van, I dropped it on the ground in front of the van, opened the door, and stood with one foot on the ground and the other foot on my gas pedal. While the van was in neutral I hit the gas. The engine roared like a snorting bull ready to run over the scooter as if it were a taunting matador. I screamed, "You better come out or I'll crush this scooter!"

Within a few seconds a large, muscular kid who appeared to be about seventeen years old came crouching out of the woods. His eyes were squinting from my headlights. He barked out, "Hey buddy, it's just me and you. Let's go!" He wanted to fight.

At that, I turned on my high beams and transformed into Jack Bauer. The light pierced his pretense and I yelled as loud as I could, "Don't jump him, men. Stand down! Don't hurt him. I think he'll cooperate!" He instantly stopped dead in his tracks. The headlights were blinding, so he placed his fingers across his eyebrows in the form of a salute and tried to see who might be coming to take him down. I yelled again, "I said stand down, boys! He's going to cooperate. There is no need to hurt him." His face shifted from angry to flat-out scared to death.

He was buying my bluff, so I decided to play it out. "Young man, put your hands in the air," I ordered. He did so instantly. "Now turn around with your back facing me," I instructed. He slowly turned around. "Take your hands and put them behind your head with your fingers in a locked position," was my next command. He did it but tried to turn his head around to see through the high beams again. I blurted out another order to my invisible legion of vandal killers, "Men, don't make any advancement toward him. We don't need to harm him. Everyone can see he is working with us!" At that he cringed—a clear indication that he was convinced that at any time my men would come out and blast him.

"Now," I said, "I want you to walk backwards toward me on my count." I gave the count, "one," and he took a step. After several more counts I had him on the ground kneeling in submission.

My wife had called the police. When the officer arrived, he saw the big teenager kneeling there in the direct path of my high beams. He asked how I managed to do that, and when I told him he laughed himself breathless. I told the cop I did not want to press charges, I only wanted the boy to be taken to his parents. When the officer told the teen the only punishment he was getting was being taken home to his parents, you would have thought we were sending him off to death row. He raised his hands in anguish and screamed, "Noooooooooooo!" I laughed out loud.

My wife told me I should have let my kids out of the van and told the boy, "Glad you did what I told you to do or these varmints would have torn you apart!" That would have been funny, but I missed the opportunity. I thank God, however, I didn't miss an opportunity that came later.

The entire van would need to be repainted and the flare kits replaced to keep it uniform in color, which made it a five thousand dollar repair. Yikes! I contacted the parents, and we talked about payment. But later that week God told me to let it go and just forgive the teenager. I called up his parents and informed them. One of the parents said, "You're kidding! This is the first good thing I have ever seen come out of anybody from the church." She was one of those people with hurting hearts. I told her that the church isn't perfect but Jesus is, and he's the one bringing about the forgiveness of the debt. I also told her how he could do that spiritually as well. She didn't respond to that, but I planted a seed, didn't I? She was grateful to be debt free, and it left her with a favorable impression of our Lord.

She wept tears of gratitude. The wine of God's forgiveness healed one more person.

Articulate what the wine of God's forgiveness means to you.

_____

_____

_____

Describe a moment in your life when you admitted your wrongdoing and how it felt during the process.

_____

_____

_____

What different emotions did you experience after you received forgiveness?

_____

_____

_____

Do you believe outsiders think Christians are forgiving? Why or why not?

_____

_____

_____

Lord Jesus, my spirit is replete with thankfulness for the forgiveness you extend to my sinning heart. The pain that comes from admitting my sin is dwarfed by the colossal joy that lifts my aching soul to soar above the hurt. Use me today to administer your wine of forgiveness. Amen.

23

Oil of Love

He who does not love does not know God, for God is love.

1 John 4:8

Oil has all kinds of uses. A fourth grade teacher informed me that her class discovered some unique places where oil is used. Here are a few I found interesting: VCR tapes, artificial turf (that explains the Atlanta Falcons' bad year), glue, electric blankets, combs (so it's not really a person's fault if his hair is oily, right?), and my personal favorite, which will go without comment, a toilet seat. The Good Samaritan also had a use for oil; he utilized it to treat a hurting man's wounds. Back at the scene of the attack:

> The ambushed victim lies fighting for his life and groaning in pain. His adrenaline helped anesthetize the injuries when they happened, but nothing is numbing the excruciating pain brought on by the alcohol that was poured into his open

> wounds. The Samaritan watches the wine enter and fill up the wounds, spilling over and carrying with it any health-threatening germs. In his weathered and worn travel pouch he also has a flask of olive oil. He pours some onto a clean piece of cloth and proceeds to carefully wipe the wounds, soothing and sealing the injuries.

I was thinking about writing another graphic description of what that moment looked like, but all this talk about gashes, blood, and germs is giving me the heebie-jeebies. I don't want to go into any more details about ancient medical procedures. Let's just say that applying the oil was the equivalent of the triple antibiotic ointments we use today. It provided a germ-fighting barrier that was critical for the wound to heal.

Do you remember my reaction to God when I was having a meltdown in my prayer closet? I was ranting about how I was exhausted and did not have the wherewithal to help people who had enormous needs. Then God responded by saying, "You have oil and wine, just like the Samaritan." With tongue in cheek I said, "What are we going to do, get drunk and get a tan?" God should have slapped me right there, but instead he gave a simple explanation. "Tony, you have the wine of forgiveness and the oil of love."

Maybe he didn't smite me because I was having another one of my ADD moments. I am a visual person, so when I heard *wine*, my mind went back to my days of getting lit on red wine. And the word *oil* had me thinking about catching some rays on the beach. When God clarified that it was the oil of love, I was instantly struck with something someone said to me after hearing my testimony. A sweet, elderly lady held my hand and said, "Love is the lotion that heals the sunburns of our souls." Love does heal.

Shortly after my conversion to Christ, I was having a really tough go at it. God had delivered me from all sorts of addictions such as alcohol, pot, pills, and cocaine. It was refreshing to wake up without the hangover those drugs gave me. Waking up without a headache was a new and welcomed moment. But eluding the headaches was one thing; escaping my heartache was another.

My heart ached with guilt from all the horrendous sins I had committed throughout my life. If my life story was a DVD, it would be rated X. The drunken rages, violent fights, and blatant debauchery had taken its toll on my mind and emotions. Although I wasn't involved in that malicious lifestyle anymore, it still haunted me. My nights were sleepless and my days were dreadful due to an inner restlessness caused by the overwhelming awareness I had of the pain my sins had caused my family and friends. I

Love is the lotion that heals the sunburns of our souls.

had stolen from others, broken the hearts of loved ones, lied to and used just about everybody I ever knew, and beaten people to a bloody mess. All the anger and hurt I had experienced in my life, I took out on everybody who otherwise could have been my friends.

One evening I was at my sister Lisa's house. When my mom remarried, she moved out and gave the house to my sister. I had a lot of battles against the forces of hell in that house, and on this night they did not want me moving on. I was in the front room looking around and recalling a moment with my dad when I realized I was sitting in the exact spot I had sat in the night my dad told Lisa and me that he was going to kill our mother. My gut was churning with the memory of the sickening feeling of fear that raped my heart that day. Suddenly I was startled out of my reflection by someone knocking on the door. I called out, "Who is it?"

"Hey man, it's me, Blake, and a couple of other guys from the church." I didn't want to see them. I was still struggling with smoking cigarettes, and I didn't need them preaching to me about quitting again. Nicotine is tough, people, and it took a miracle that I received a month later to deliver me from it. On this night, unknown to me or even the guys that were bringing it, I was going to get another miracle.

"Be right there," I replied as I ran to the bathroom and sprayed on some cheap Stetson cologne to cover up the smell of smoke. After twenty squirts, I opened the door. A cold rush of crisp March air greeted me along with the strong handshakes of my visitors.

"Hey man, we're just out visiting people who have visited the church, and tonight we thought you could use a visit." My pre-conversion Tony was screaming within me, "I don't need a visit, so why don't you guys get away from my house!" I didn't say it out loud, but those words were caged in my heart, growling like an insane pit bull, viciously snapping its sharp teeth at their approach. I was angry with myself for being such a sinful person and at the habit I had created of hurting those who wanted to help me. Such is the cycle of those enslaved to sin. But I was about to be reminded that I had been set free.

I wasn't up for a church talk visit so I just sat there and let my ears work but never made an effort to listen. The devil had a strong, negative hold on my heart, and besides that, what I did hear I didn't like. Do you remember those guns of holiness that I mentioned in a previous chapter—the ones we are often quick to use to shoot out our distaste for the conduct of outsiders? Well, two of these guys pulled them out and started popping caps at me. The first thing out of their mouths was a harsh interrogation: "You haven't been to church in a couple of weeks. Where were you?" They concluded that my absence meant I wasn't living up to what I told God I would do when I gave him my life. Their judgmental tone convinced me that I couldn't trust them with the shameful confession that I was in my bathroom Sunday morning with a gun to my head wrestling with the demons of regret.

After a few more interrogating questions like, "Have you been reading your Bible and praying every day?" "When are you going to get baptized?" and, "I smell smoke. Are you still smoking?" I checked out. *Where are my smokes anyway? I sure could use one*, I thought to myself. After about thirty minutes of subjecting me to their spiritual waterboarding, one of the guys said, "We better head out before it gets too late." At that I got spiritual: *Finally. Hallelujah!*

As we stood up to head toward the door, one of the visitors did something to me that I had never experienced in my life. He faced me and held both sides of my face in his hands. He was a strange-looking fellow who resembled actor Kevin Spacey wearing Napoleon Dynamite's glasses. His name was Kilby. He was an unpopular, odd, quiet person in the College and Singles Ministry. He may not have had many friends, but he was God's buddy and full of the Spirit. During the whole evening he had not said a single word. He just sat there smiling at me. Now he was cradling my face with his hands and staring at me from behind the biggest set of glasses I have ever seen on a man.

Everybody in the room froze, including me. As he stared at me, he slowly tilted his head to both sides the way my dog does when I whistle softly. His eyes swelled with tears that were magnified by the thickness of his spectacles. At that moment, a heat seared from his hands and it shot through my entire body. A surreal feeling of calm started radiating from deep within my being as Kilby spoke. His voice was as odd as his demeanor; it was deep and low like R&B soul singer Barry White. With a wide, inviting smile Kilby said, "God loves you, baby!"

While the other guys' faces clearly showed contempt for Kilby's actions, I melted in approval. It was unorthodox; it was strange and out-of-the-box. He didn't even know me, but it was of the Spirit and it was a message from God to me. While the other guys were thinking they were on a mission from God to size me up, God couldn't wait for them to shut up so he could use Kilby to seize me up with his love! I was drowning in the raging river of regrets, and God lifted me up and placed me into his lifeboat of love.

It's been years since that evening, and I am still fueled by that moment. God's message of love healed me deeply that day. After hearing my testimony, thousands of people have written me or visited me at my table during one of our tour stops and have asked how I have made it through so much pain. My response is always the same: "Love wins!" God's love has soothed the wounds of my heart and has provided a barrier to keep out the

> **I was drowning in the raging river of regrets, and God lifted me up and placed me into his lifeboat of love.**

demons of my past and the hurtful actions of others that happen from time to time. And he has done the same for countless others.

As I have traveled and spoken in major arenas in most of the biggest cities in our country, I have had the privilege of ministering to millions of people. I am no expert, but like you, I can make observations. And my observations have told me that the two biggest needs people have are to be relieved of their guilt and to be really loved. The awesome thing for a hurt healer is that we have the remedies for both of those pains—forgiveness and love.

D E L V E

If love is the lotion that can heal the sunburns of our souls, what blisters of yours have been healed by God's love?

_____

_____

_____

Pretend you are having a discussion with an outsider who feels rejected by Christians. Write out how you would describe the oil of God's love.

_____

_____

_____

Review what you just read and ask God to bring someone into your path today who needs to hear it. Be ready to share.

_____

_____

_____

Lord, you are love. As I am convinced of this, others will be also. Help me to be like Kilby and take a daring risk to share the oil of your love with someone who desperately needs it. Amen.

24

Give Back Good

But the fruit of the Spirit is love, joy, peace, longsuffering, kindness, goodness, faithfulness, gentleness, self-control.

Galatians 5:22–23

To start this chapter out, I need to ask a question that will require serious consideration. Do you believe the last sentence I wrote in chapter 23? As hurt healers, we have the remedies for the pains of guilt and feeling unloved— forgiveness and love. If we believe this, we can be a different representation of Jesus to those who have an unfavorable impression of him and his church. Think about the reality of what I am proposing. If the two biggest needs of most hurting people are to be relieved of their guilt and to really be loved, then a hurt healer can be and should be a hero to them. Like when Dr. Phil humbles the hurtful husband and causes him to turn from his hateful ways, or like the caregiver in the orphanage in Nanchong who cradles the crying infant for hours in aching arms of love until the baby slips off into dreamland, we have what they need—forgiveness and love.

I love history. But to be honest, I don't like reading about it because I get lost in the numbers and dates. I don't do numbers like my father-in-law doesn't do blood. It's one of the reasons I'm terrible at golf. I have a sweet swing, if I do say so myself, but I lose it when it comes to picking the number of a club that will hit the ball a certain way. I also can't keep score at all. Whose idea was it to have the smallest number win anyway?

> **As hurt healers, we have the remedies for the pains of guilt and feeling unloved— forgiveness and love.**

Let me get back to history. A history professor told a story about an altercation that occurred between the German soldiers of East and West Berlin. I don't know if the story is true, but if it is, it was a grand moment.

West Germany was known as the Federal Republic of Germany. It was a Western capitalist country with a social market economy and a democratic parliamentary government. East Germany, or the German Democratic Republic, had an authoritarian government with a Soviet-style planned economy. Americans tend to say that the West was free and the East was Communist. Berlin was divided into two sides, which were separated by a large wall. The civilians of the East desired freedom, and those who tried to escape over the wall into West Berlin often lost their lives by the rifle fire of an East Berlin soldier. It was a hostile and charged border.

One cold, snowy day in December 1962, many of the East Berlin Grepo soldiers were still very angry over the news caused earlier that year when they shot Peter Fechter in full view of the West Berlin media as he tried to escape. He did not die from the initial shot, but none of the Grepos went to his aid. Instead they let him lie there and slowly bleed to death. The world witnessed that event through photos taken by West Berliners. East Germany was trying to convince the

170   SHOWING JESUS

world that their way of living was the best way, and the photos of the shooting set them back considerably. Hostilities between the two sides intensified.

Several East Berlin soldiers decided to pull a nasty prank on the West Berlin soldiers who held positions at a guard shack near the wall. The East soldiers gathered several hundred pounds of garbage from the waste fields outside the city. Rotting foods, soiled bathroom tissues, and road kill were gathered in a large hydraulic dump truck. In the middle of the night while the West Berlin soldiers were sound asleep in their shelter, the East Berlin soldiers dumped the maggot-infested, filthy gift over onto the West side of the wall just outside the shelter.

The next morning the West soldiers tried to exit their lodging and could not due to the trash that was piled up six feet high outside their door. Once they got the door open, the smell of rotting garbage reeked repugnantly through the air. It took days to clean up and weeks for the nauseating smell to dissipate.

Later, as the West Berlin soldiers played a game of cards one evening, a payback was planned. Smelling his wool coat, one of the soldiers yelled, "My clothes still smell of decomposed rabbit. Let's get those Grepos back!" "Yeah!" another joined in. It didn't take long for everyone to fold in on the card game as the room filled with shouts of retaliation. They decided they would get even with the East Berlin soldiers in a way they would never forget. They worked all night on it.

When the sun rose, the East Berliners began coming out of their barracks sipping their coffee, trying to shake the morning cobwebs from their heads and chase away the early chill. The West Berlin soldiers watched their movements through binoculars from an empty apartment window that gave them a perch to view activity over the wall. One Grepo was lighting his cigarette when he noticed something large next to the wall near their guardhouse. He slapped the soldier next to him, who was still struggling to rid the sleep from his eyes.

The heap before them indicated they had another visitor as well.

The soldiers approached the mass with eyes wide and jaws dropped. Its enormous size seemed to induce a trance that made them drop their coffee and smokes, which smoldered in the snow near their combat boots. Two tons of imperishable food items such as canned meats and soups were neatly stacked in the shape of a large pyramid. Glimmering in the beams of the morning sunrise was a note that had been placed on top of the stack. The soldier who saw it first raced up the mountain of nourishment, grabbed it, and read it out loud for all to hear. The hearts of the East Berliners sank in deep conviction as they heard, "Each side gives what each side has to give."

Up in their perch, the West Berliners put down their binoculars, looking to one another with smiles of approval and shaking their comrades' hands for a job well done.

When I was developing this chapter, I thought this story carried great relevance to another battle taking place. I hang out with a lot of Christians, but I also have friendships with a lot of non-Christians. It's not a news flash when I tell you that a huge wall separates Christians and non-Christians. Great hostilities exist between the two worlds, and over the years a lot of trash has been thrown from both sides. I know Christians want unbelievers to stop heaping up their garbage in our lives and minds; I don't like the garbage either. My understanding of Scripture tells me they are sinners, but that does not give them a ticket to bash us and flaunt their filth all they want because they can't help themselves.

I remember, however, what it was like to be enslaved to my sin and regularly hurt people. I am not trying to degrade them, but the reality is that they give what they have to give. I suggest that believers in Jesus should offer something entirely different in return. Scripture tells us that we have the stuff of God to politely and lovingly put back in their court. We have the fruits of the Spirit: love, joy, peace, patience, kindness,

172   SHOWING JESUS

goodness, gentleness, faithfulness, and self-control. We also have a supply line from God that gives us everything we need for life and godliness. To top that off, the Bible says we can do all things through the strength of Christ. This tells me there is hope for a better relationship between the two groups of people. But when will it start to show? When will Christians return good for garbage?

Writing this chapter, I feel a little like Ronald Reagan when he stood outside Brandenburg Gate on June 12, 1987, and challenged Soviet Premier Mikhail Gorbachev to liberate the Soviet bloc nations, saying, "Mr. Gorbachev, tear down this wall!" It was a big request from the Gipper, but that wall did get torn down. It's also a big request from God to us.

When will Christians return good for garbage?

I'd like to expound on another thing that I have learned from Scripture. In Ephesians 2, Paul deals with a dividing wall that existed between Jews and Greeks; he says that God through Christ has broken down that wall. The sacrificial death of Jesus on the cross detonates and obliterates the sin that divides. Do you realize what great news that is to this world? Do you grasp what that means for broken homes, tension-filled friendships, drug-infested neighborhoods, suicidal teenagers, disillusioned millionaires, and hate-filled churches? It's astonishingly good news! The gospel of Jesus Christ says that life should be and can be different because hurt healers have the capacity to give the imperishable gifts of love and forgiveness to the thug, the whore, the killer, the lawyer, the ex-wife, the stepchild, the hateful boss, the bully, the person popping up in your mind right now who has done you wrong or hurt you deeply.

When they give spin, we give truth.
When they give death, we give life.
When they give theft, we give generously.

When they give lust, we give modesty.
When they give gossip, we give a kind word.
When they give mistreatment, we give a second mile.
When they give grudges, we give forgiveness.
And when they give hate, we give love!

The only thing we should never be seen giving is *giving up*. Can I ask you to please never give up at being a hurt healer? They need us.

I've spoken with the mom who sat on the back row of church while the members gave her stares to quiet down her child who hadn't stopped crying since dad walked out. I've prayed with the thief who is haunted by the feeling that he will never serve enough time to pay back the life he stole. I've tried to think for a boy who lost his mind on meth after trying it only one time. I've counseled the millionaire who is sickened that he spent his life pursuing the most expensive things one could purchase but in the process lost all the things you can't buy. I've held the hand of a sick widow who would rather die than spend another day alone. I've cried with the unwed, pregnant teenager whose whole life is changed forever because of a brief moment of weakness.

> **Please never give up at being a hurt healer. They need us.**

I have to say it again. They need us! I know they do. They've told me so. They tell me so every day through their emails and phone calls. Please listen to me. I've walked more than a mile in the shoes of the druggie, the drunk, the depressed, the derelict, the damaged, and the deranged. And my million-mile journey with them has taken me to this moment right now on this page with you. Will you please, for the sake of love, dare to live an extraordinary life of being a hurt healer for them?

Let's be different. Let's give back good. What happens when you do will be surprising and amazing.

D E L V E

Explain what it means to you to be relieved of your guilt.

_____

_____

_____

How would you describe to someone what it feels like to be really loved?

_____

_____

_____

What are you prepared to toss over the wall between you and the outsiders in your world?

_____

_____

_____

When I say, "They need us," what are you hearing me say?

_____

_____

_____

Dear Lord, you are the great wall destroyer. Through your power and the fruits of the Spirit, help me to offer back to this hurting world something different than what they have thrown at me. May I give my all but never give up. Amen.

25

Thumbs-Up!

> But even after we had suffered before and were spitefully
> treated at Philippi, as you know, we were bold in our God to
> speak to you the gospel of God in much conflict.
>
> 1 Thessalonians 2:2

I vividly recall the night God invited me to be a hurt healer.
It happened about six months after my conversion and was
a defining moment that I never saw coming. Life was going
great for me. I was still basking in the warmth of God's love
that had overwhelmed me through the face-grab from God's
buddy, Kilby. God was providing odd jobs for me to do that
kept me fed and the bills paid. I was starting to develop new
friendships in the church, and I was enjoying the blessings
of being set free from a self-sabotaging lifestyle. I was also
full of dreams of what my new life in Christ could look like.
Little did I know I was about to be informed.

The sun had just set and the Florida sky was afire with brilliant pinks and calming cascades of violets amid a warming glow of bronze. I had just rounded a corner in my Volkswagen van and pressed my knee against the steering wheel, freeing up both of my hands, which I stuck out the window toward heaven and applauded God for his freshly painted sunset. Ten minutes later I noticed a partial reflection of myself in the rearview mirror, and it revealed I was smiling. I remembered how many times I had looked in a mirror during my lifetime, and all I'd seen was a pitifully sad, frowning face filled with hurt.

The radio had been playing, but I hadn't noticed any particular songs. Then all of a sudden it was as if someone turned up the volume, but nobody was in the van with me. Just then God's voice pressed in on my spirit and softly said, "Listen."

Dramatic piano tones danced with crying violins, and the melodious voice of Babbie Mason seeped into my heart through her song "Show Me How to Love."[1] It's a soul-stirring ballad about the plight of hurting humanity and the beckoning cry of God for us to do something about it.

In the song, the sight of an abused, homeless, and hungry single mother and her family has caused the singer to tune in to the voice of God. His voice is soft and compassionate. He is asking a question, and it's one that would change my heart and life forever, one right out of the heart of Jesus in Matthew 25: "What will you do for the least of these?" God wants to know what the songwriter intends to do about the brokenness she sees in this pain-filled world.

With both hands now on the wheel, I quickly looked for a place to pull over. I could hear the heart of God through this song, and I knew he wanted to use it to speak to me in a way that would have eternal significance. I screeched into the parking lot of an abandoned warehouse—a shell of a building with broken windows and weathered paint that seemed to represent the empty lives the song was speaking about.

The music continued as the strings seemed to wail and beg in unison with the enchanting vocalist, and suddenly I sensed God directly questioning me as to what my response would be to the hurt I see happening all around me. I began to weep openly. A surge of warmth radiated within my heart. It was as if I was leaning against the chest of God and could hear his heartbeat for those he came to die for. Then, in a strange yet authentically supernatural moment, it was as if God began implanting or downloading his compassion into my heart as the singer's voice swelled and she begged God to help her love the hurting with no regard for personal gain. I found myself covering my face with both of my hands, and they were filled with the wet evidence of a heart that could feel deeply for others. I joined Babbie Mason in her transparent request as I asked God to help me be someone who authentically loved others. I caught God's heart that night through that song, and I set out to be a hurt healer. Little did I know what would await me.

I naively thought that everybody would love a hurt healer. But sadly, when I told you that a lot of tension exists at the great divide between the world of those who hurt and those who can heal the hurt, it's because I've experienced it. I was not prepared to deal with the trash throwing and the hostilities that hurt healers are subjected to. If you decide to be someone who seeks to love and expect nothing in return, let me forewarn you that you will get something in return all right.

For example, one of the colorful personalities I hung out with in my neighborhood was a pothead named Ray. He had long, brown hair that he wore in a ponytail that went all the way down to his waist. Ray was a typical dude from Sin City. He smoked pot from sunup to sundown. He hardly worked, but when he did, he worked hard. He carried a gun, but the attitude he carried was worse, so he never had to use it. Oddly enough, Ray loved to laugh; he was one of the funniest guys I have ever met. He was busting redneck jokes long before Jeff Foxworthy. He was the jester among the rogues in our ghetto. But one day after my conversion, I had a run-in with Ray that was no laughing matter.

I didn't hang out by the fire with these guys anymore because after I got saved, I stopped drinking and smoking pot. They assumed I thought I was now too good to hang out with them. One blistering summer day, Ray approached me, and his face indicated that his anger was hotter than the weather. "You don't party with us anymore, Nolan," he said with an indicting grin. Then the whole motley crew of about seven other dudes yelled a few incriminating words.

If you decide to be someone who seeks to love and expect nothing in return, let me forewarn you that you will get something in return all right.

I calmly replied, "Yeah, guys, Jesus changed my life, and I'm just not into it anymore." What happened next blew my mind. Ray took the beer bottle he had in his hand and smashed it across the deck rail. It shattered, and he was now wielding the broken end of it toward my neck.

His eyes were bloodshot from drinking and filled with the hatred of a thousand demons. I just stood there and faced him eye-to-eye as he screamed, "F— you and your —— God!" He was drunk, and I knew I could swiftly snap his wrist, take that sharp glass, and do surgery on his derrière with it. But God spoke to me and said, "Walk away."

As I slowly made my way up the street, they dumped their verbal trash all over me. "Yeah, walk away, sissy!" "You better leave, Christian punk, or we'll gut you!" I lowered my head trying to hide the tears. I wanted to retaliate, but the Spirit of God in me was praying for their souls, and I found myself moving beyond the hurt I was experiencing and instead hurting for them. Over the next several months as I worked among those guys, they kept up their daily abuse. I so much wanted to fight back, but God pressed me to love the unlovable.

So I found another way to retaliate. When I saw one of the guys was a little short on money, I privately slipped him a twenty-dollar bill. He barked a cuss word at me but took the money anyway, commenting that Christians were stupid and weak, giving up their money like a child succumbing to a bully. But I knew I was giving it out of the power of God and in a spirit of love. Regularly, one of them showed up at my doorstep drunk and bloody from a fight, and I'd let him sleep on my couch. The next morning, I would already be gone when he woke, but he'd find a hot plate of breakfast waiting for him and a twenty dollar bill in his pocket. They never acknowledged the gifts, but they always made a point to cuss me out in front of their buddies.

I will be honest with you right here: I did not want to keep this up, especially when they made jokes that I could not laugh at anymore about God and his church. I often felt like Jesus's disciples who wanted to call down fire and watch them all turn into little crispy critters. I was ready to throw in the towel and call it quits, buy a small, semiautomatic handgun, and give them a convincing argument that God is real by putting them into his presence. Then one day the unlikely happened.

I was waxing the top of my van because it was rusted out and the wax filled the holes where it leaked when it rained. I remember it was so hot outside that the wax melted when it touched the surface. I had my radio on, and it was busting out some sweet early nineties Michael W. Smith when Ray walked up. He had not approached me since our altercation a year ago. I was blessed to have walked away from that moment because he always finished every fight he started. I braced myself thinking that's what he had come to do. He looked at my radio and made an "I'm going to hurl" face, opening up his mouth and sticking out his tongue. He was joking, but he wasn't joking. He reached into his pocket, and I quickly looked around for a screwdriver to use, thinking he was getting a knife. But there wasn't a screwdriver around. Then Ray stuck his other hand in his other pocket. That was odd. You don't fight with both of your hands in your pockets.

Ray kept his face toward the ground for a very long time. Michael W. Smith's song provided the score for the drama that was unfolding. Ray slowly looked up at me on my ladder. His eyes were bloodshot, but this time it was because he had not had a drink in over a week. (Later I heard that he and his wife had had a fight and the authorities got involved because a child got hurt. So Ray was trying to dry out.) Water leaked from the corners of his eyes. Grief and regret shaped his quivering face. He kept his eyes fixed to mine as he started walking away. He raised one of his hands up out of his pocket and gave me a thumbs-up. His voice almost didn't work, finding it difficult to speak past the frog in his throat. When it did come out, it was breathy and squeaky with emotion, "I'm for you, Tony."

Ray had been watching to see how I would respond to his maltreatment. He knew my background. He knew my emotions were like a bottle of nitroglycerin and it didn't take much to make me explode with anger. He had a similar story, and it fueled his daily rages. When he saw that I gave back good, it convinced his heart of the authenticity of my conversion and the ability of Jesus to be mighty to save. He came to offer a peace treaty, and from my ladder I invited him to receive the Prince of Peace. "Ray, Jesus loves you. He is the one who has been loving on you guys through me. I couldn't do that, Ray. I wanted to kill you, bro, but Jesus is real, and he can do for you what he's done for me. He can heal your hurts, Ray!"

Without a word, he made a motion with his lips that said, "I know." I watched him walk to his truck and drive away. As he drove off, he kept his thumb up out of the window all the way down the road until he was out of sight. Michael W. Smith's song filled the air: "Great Is the Lord!"

This is the mission of a hurt healer, and we can accomplish it if we are willing to endure the hostilities and let our actions speak as loud as our words. I saw Ray recently when I was home preaching for a funeral of a relative. He was cleaned up and sober, sitting in the crowd. As I gave the eulogy of our mutual loved one, he looked up at me and gave me that thumbs-up again. I looked for him at the graveside, but we never connected. I don't know if Ray has ever received Christ, but his thumbs-up was the equivalent to the psalmist's declaration, "Taste and see that the Lord is good and blessed are those who trust in God" (Ps. 34:8).

> *We can accomplish our mission if we are willing to endure the hostilities and let our actions speak as loud as our words.*

D E L V E

What thoughts went through your mind after you read the lines in Babbie's song that say, "Open up my eyes that I might really see more and more of you and less of me by loving the unlovable and touching the untouchable. Let my actions speak much louder than my words!"

_____

_____

_____

Have you ever been attacked for living out your faith? How did it make you feel?

_____

_____

_____

In what way does the story about Ray inspire you to keep the faith?

_____

_____

_____

Jesus, you know what it was like to be forsaken and rejected because of the faith. O Lord, thank you that you know what that feels like and understand my trembling heart. I offer up the reproach that I endure as an act of worship to you. May I hold onto the idea and hope that one day those who attack might return to give you praise. Amen.

26

Divine Props

And behold, I am coming quickly, and My reward is with
Me, to give to every one according to his work.

Revelation 22:12

Did I tell you that Ray looked like Jesus? Through paint-
ings, murals, and movies with actors depicting Jesus, we all
have a pretty similar idea of what he looked like: Jewish guy
with protruding cheekbones, oversized eyes, a short beard,
and the signature long, brown hair. If you have this idea of
what Jesus looked like, you also have a picture of my buddy
Ray. When I was preaching that funeral and saw Ray out in
the crowd, I thought to myself, "Hello, Jesus. I'm glad you
could make it." As I reflect about Ray giving me a thumbs-
up, I immediately get a picture of Jesus giving props out to
the Good Samaritan.

Jesus stands at the bottom of a large hill. He has chosen the position knowing that the sound of his voice will travel up the side of the knoll, making it easier for people to hear him. The slope also enables the listener to have a full view of him. Taking another drink from his water jug, Jesus scans the top of the ridge. The people closest to him notice that although he is taking a drink, he appears to be looking for someone. Several of them turn their necks and canvass the crowd, wondering who he is searching for.

Jesus's eyes light up and he smiles while still taking his sip, causing the cool water to leak from the spout and trickle down his beard. His eyes have found their target. Still smiling, he wipes his drenched mouth and looks back at the crowd. Many of them are hot and tired, but their faces show determination to forego shade so they can see this face-off to the finish. The lawyer just answered Jesus's question about who the neighbor in the story is by shouting back, "He who showed mercy on him!" Now Jesus is about to finish off the attorney, give the world a great commission, and encourage a very deserving Samaritan.

"Go and do likewise!" cheers the Lord.

Don't think you are alone in feeling odd about this idea of Jesus cheering. The crowd was a bit confused as well. Wasn't Jesus supposed to smash his opponent with a riveting rebuttal while pointing a rebuking finger in his face? That's what we would do, right? Instead, Jesus's voice is full of celebration, and his finger isn't even pointed in the direction of the lawyer. He is pointing to the top of the ridge. What's on the ridge? Well, it's not what's on the ridge, but who. It's our Hurt Healer!

Jesus's face is overcome with emotion as he stands there, arm extended and finger directed at the Good Samaritan. The moment sort of resembles a scene in the movie *Jerry Maguire* where Tom Cruise points at famed football player

Rod Tidwell, who is surrounded by reporters asking him what it felt like to win a Monday night football game with an amazing catch in the end zone. Jesus is smiling, yet his eyes are streaming with tears of sheer appreciation and applause as he gestures to the Samaritan. Good job, you rock, attaboy, you are the man!

But there are no reporters surrounding the Samaritan. Remember, he is an outcast. He isn't welcome company among the purebred Jews. So he is off in the distance standing on top of a haystack with his hands cupped behind his ears honing in on Jesus's every word. From the top of the ridge he can hardly believe what he's hearing. Jesus isn't calling him a half-breed; he isn't pointing at him to go away. Jesus is throwing him some divine props! Jesus is cheering his good conduct.

Jesus's voice of approval is a thumbs-up, clearly communicating to the Samaritan and all who are listening, "I am celebrating this good man's great achievement of making a difference in a hurting heart so that every human being throughout the ages will emulate his conduct." This has to be the best day of this guy's life!

I craved approval my whole life until I met Jesus. Since my dad told me I wasn't worth two hundred dollars and that I would never amount to anything, I found myself far off from the crowd many times, cupping my ears for any word that would tell me I mattered. I remember all too well what that felt like. So when I read that Jesus gave a shout-out to this lowly Samaritan, I wept and celebrated with him. I imagine the hammers in his ears dancing instead of beating on his eardrums, sending the never-before-heard message to his heart: "You matter!" I picture him loosening the belt around his emotionally starved stomach as it bulges from feasting on Jesus's all-you-can-eat buffet of belonging. His heart, clogged with the plaque of worthlessness, begins to freely beat again as it is catheterized by the significance of being used as the poster child for what it looks like to live out the second commandment.

And to think that this kind of moment awaits every hurt healer! One day we will see Jesus face-to-face. In the same way that he saw the activity of the Samaritan's life, he is watching ours. He sees when you visit the prisoner in jail; he views our secret deeds for the poor; he notices every time we stand up for him and get knocked down by others. Yes, the story of the Good Samaritan challenges us. But oh, dear reader, let your heart be filled with joyful anticipation as well. One day we will be in Christ's presence, and the Bible tells us that he will say to those who have served him in fumbling, frail, yet fortified faith, "Well done, good and faithful servant." How rich will that moment be? I dream about that day.

> *In the same way that Jesus saw the activity of the Samaritan's life, he is watching ours.*

In my dream, I see Jesus standing there with the same smile he had for the Samaritan stretching across his face. His arms are wide open, inviting me to come and get the hug I have been waiting for since I met him. Wrapped in his arms, my entire being is drenched in the same warmth that radiated my body that night Kilby cradled my face. I melt. It's over! The fighting, the flesh, and the warring against the devil and his host of demons has finally ended. I am home! I see Jesus take me by my shoulders, and kindly push me back, and stare into my eyes. He holds my face in his hands and says, "I love you, baby!" I feel the scars on his hands as he touches my cheeks—proof of the love he professes. He closes his eyes as if tracing a memory. He is reviewing my life.

I shudder shamefully, remembering the millions of things I have done that displeased him. I close my eyes now and brace myself for a warranted reproof. I feel his hands tighten around my face. I am waiting, but there is nothing. I sheepishly open my eyes and see that Jesus's eyes are now fully open, staring directly into mine. His lip curves up to one side and he looks at me like a parent about to correct a child. I know a rebuke is imminent. Then to my utter amazement, Jesus busts out a belly-shaking laugh!

His eyes are full of the things we dream of seeing in the eyes of those we look up to—love, acceptance, approval, and trust. I am caught up in the moment; my eyes begin to gush tears of elation. I can't seem to catch my breath, but I have never been so full of life! I'm in heaven and I'm with Jesus. I was sure I would be ashamed, but it's just the opposite as I hear Jesus sing a celebrating, intoxicating song: "Well done, Tony, my good and faithful servant." He is singing it! I thought he was just supposed to say it, and I thought I would never hear it because I know I am undeserving. But *he is singing it* over me!

"This is heaven!" I shout, and I shake my face free from his grasp and fall to the ground kissing his battle wounds from Calvary. I can't stop kissing his feet, and I weep and weep. I am astounded because I am actually experiencing the message I have heard and have given about Jesus—that we are forgiven, really forgiven from the moment of salvation for every sin we commit. And now it is unveiling before my very eyes. God, who has seen all my failures and blemishes, is actually pleased with me. And when I thought that I had failed him by not accomplishing great big things for him, I am elated to discover that he is bonkers over the things I did for his glory!

He is still singing, and it's loud, and now all of heaven is joining in. They have never stopped rejoicing that this sinner got saved, and now they are shaking the foundations of heaven because God is pleased. This is love, this is joy, and oh, the hope it brings to know it will be forever.

Not too long ago I had the honor of being the road pastor and gospel preacher for Casting Crowns on their Lifesong Tour. I loved that tour. Friendships were forged and my faith was fueled by the ladies and men in that band. The band members love Jesus, and some other Jesus lovers joined us— Nichole Nordeman and Building 429. We held a worship service every Sunday when we were on the road. We praised the Lord together, and then I preached a brief message. God

188

was faithful to give us a word to keep us dialed in to his heart for the kingdom. A lot of this book was birthed out of a message I gave on one of those Sundays.

All of the artists are Dove Award winners, which is a coveted achievement marking grand accomplishments in the Christian music industry. After preaching the message on the Good Samaritan, I humbly offered them a challenge: "Don't seek the Dove Award; instead seek the *above reward*." There is nothing wrong with having a Dove Award. Shine 'em if ya got 'em. My point was that those little brass statues will decay, and fame on earth is fleeting. There is an everlasting award when God above looks down on our activities below and says about our conduct, "Go and do likewise."

Man, keep the Grammys, the Oscars, and the Doves. Hearing, "Go and do likewise," from the mouth of Jesus has to be the supreme accolade, and the reward that comes with it is eternal.

D E L V E

Try to remember a time when you received praise for a job well done. Write out three to five of the feelings you experienced as a result of that moment.

_____

_____

Knowing that one day God will celebrate your achievements, great or small, how should that affect the way you conduct yourself daily?

_____

_____

_____

Make a list of the awards you have received in your life, large and small.

_____

_____

_____

Can any of them compare to the reward of God giving you props in heaven for being a hurt healer for his kingdom purposes?

_____

_____

_____

God, help me to live like I'm leaving and you are coming. One day I will be in your presence, and each moment in your presence will become my newest great moment. Just hearing you sing over me with joy will be enough reward to last me throughout all eternity. Today I will live and treat others with that in mind. Amen.

27

Picking Locked Hearts

The king's heart is in the hand of the LORD, like the rivers of water; He turns it wherever He wishes.

Proverbs 21:1

Evangelistic hurt healers are often met with resistance from people within the church. My journey with God took me from living in a van to going to Bible college to study for ministry. I know that may seem like a quantum leap—it was. That's kind of the way it goes when you upgrade *your* version of living for *God's* way of living. When I was in college, I worked at several churches. If your mind was a wireless network that allowed you to have access to my memories, then you would see file after file that would show intense clashes with people who opposed my hurt healing efforts. Actually, my thoughts written in this book may give you access to some of those files. Let me thumb through a few of them. Ah . . . there it is—the Locklake file. Together let's check out the memory of one of my experiences at that church.

Locklake Baptist Church should have been more appropriately called Locked Hearts Baptist Church. They hired me to share the gospel and serve the youth as a minister of evangelism and of students. Serving their teenagers really meant that the parents wanted me to fix them in one hour of small groups and send them home easier to deal with. They also didn't want me to actually evangelize others. They just wanted to have someone on staff called an evangelist so they could look better than the other churches in the area. Perhaps they did want me to share the gospel, as long as it meant they didn't have to do it and the people we reached acted like them, smelled like them, and had their same skin color.

Evangelistic hurt healers are often met with resistance from people within the church.

To say that I had some serious conflicts there would be an understatement. It was hell in the midst of a place that was supposed to be helping people get to heaven. But my heart broke for those people. I served with a passion, believing God could break through their self-absorbed hearts. I wanted to believe that they could get over themselves and start caring about the hurting people around them who desperately needed humanitarian aid and just as desperately needed the salvation Christians have to offer. I'm a pretty fired-up guy, but I had experiences there that almost extinguished my flame.

In an effort to reach people who were far from God so they could be captured by God's great love, I decided to host a special "bring a friend" day. Our auditorium held 500 people, but the most they ever had was 250. I worked hard to make this day a success, and it ended up being amazing—filled with exhilarating worship and the Word of God that compassionately invited people to receive Jesus and challenged believers to share Christ with others. We actually had over 500 in attendance, and people responded to the gospel invitation! I was jazzed until I got a call later that afternoon from

192   **SHOWING JESUS**

one of my staff friends who said the deacons were holding an emergency meeting to fire me. Can you believe that? Like I said, they should have been called Locked Hearts.

I was ready to head to the church, empty my desk, and quit when God spoke: "Go to the meeting."

I said, "For what, so they can fire me to my face?"

His reply sent a chill up my back that let me know I was going to experience something otherworldly: "I want you to see something."

I made a call to our administrator to ensure that I could attend the meeting. He checked the deacon procedure material and gave me the go-ahead. I called up some of my friends who served on staff with me and told them I was going, and they all agreed to go with me. Now I would have some backup by my side.

When we walked through the door, I felt like I was in an old western movie, busting in like Clint Eastwood on a gang of outlaws planning a lynching. However, when we lunged into the room, the deacons were not a bit impressed or intimidated. They had their rope, and somebody was going to swing.

God spoke again: "Sit down, silly!" I went for the closest chair while my boys spread out around the large business table. We were outnumbered four to twelve, but I was about to learn we were not outpowered.

The deacons picked up where they were before we made our pitiful, gunslinger entrance. One of them shouted, "Today was a catastrophe, and we, as the leaders, must ensure that it never happens again!"

I wanted to scream, "You guys aren't leaders; deacons are servants!" but couldn't because another deacon yelled, "Yeah, this is an outrage!"

For the next thirty minutes they all shouted their distaste for me and the ministry I was conducting at the church. I had shamed them and brought a blight on their fellowship. How? I was guilty of bringing in the homeless and African-

Americans who came forward for salvation. I was outraged and begged God to rain down large hailstones of fire on them as long as I could get out of the building first.

Throughout the thirty-minute barrage of accusations, I tried to speak up for myself. But God kept saying, "Shh! Don't say a word. I'm going to show you something."

Then in a very surreal moment, everyone quit yelling and turned their necks and stared me down. Their eyes were like darts, spears, guns, and knives. I was ready to jump across the table and bust some "before-Jesus Tony" on them. Suddenly the silence was broken as one of the men stood up and yelled, "What's all this nit-picking?" Every head turned slowly in unison away from me and fixed their attention on Lewis Newman. He was a very handsome seventy-year-old who was always dressed well and kept his brilliant, white, wavy hair combed perfectly. His face was smooth and almost wrinkle-free. He was just one of those beautiful people you hope to be when you get old. He was even more beautiful on the inside and was revered as the godliest man in our church.

I was surprised to see Lewis at the meeting, but I figured he was just another hypocrite. I was wrong. His old finger shaking with tension and his voice cracking with age in holy anger, he shouted again, "Tell me, what's all this nit-picking?"

God nudged me again. "Tony, I am going to show you that I know how to pick a locked heart."

Mr. Newman slammed both of his fists on the table, which I thought was going to break his elderly bones, and he said, "I stormed the beaches of Normandy, men, and I was just a religious man. If I would have died like most of my friends did that day, I would have gone to hell as a good church member. I thank God this boy wants to make sure people are prepared for death and that their souls are saved. What's all this nit-picking?"

Silence filled the room for about two awkward minutes. I thought to myself, *What is going to happen now? Will they erupt in a revolt and hang Lewis with me?* Just then the head deacon stood up and took his coat off. I didn't want him to stand up. He was a massive, three-hundred-pound strong state trooper who could snap me in half with his fingers. His face was red, and he looked like he was about to explode. He flipped his coat over his shoulder and said, "This meeting is over, gentlemen." I was stunned as his lips began to tremble and tears began to slide down his face. "I'm convicted; truth is I'm angry at myself. I know I should be sharing my faith, but I haven't. Then Tony shows up caring and sharing Jesus. I should be rejoicing but instead I am angry. Something is wrong with me, and something is wrong with all of us. I am not going to let us fire him and empower us to keep on living like we shouldn't." He turned toward me with his face tight and eyes bloodshot from repressing his emotions. "I've got a brother-in-law I've known for over twenty years. I love him, but I have never shared the gospel with him. I'm going to see him right now. Meeting's over, boys!" He smiled at me and walked out.

God spoke again. "How cool is that, Tony? I won this fight and never had to throw a punch. Keep sharing the gospel, son, and I will pick the locked hearts of sinners and saints alike."

> **God will use your example to fling open the locked hearts of those who are indifferent.**

Hurt healers, you will face resistance when you decide to take the high road and be different from the hurtful heretics in your church. Stay the course, use restraint, and God will show you something utterly otherworldly and entirely life changing. He will raise up other hurt healers like Mr. Newman who will join ranks with you and not let the real atrocity of religious pride get in the way of a needy soul's salvation. God will use your example to fling open the locked hearts of those who are indifferent. He did it for me, and I know he did it through the example of the Good Samaritan.

Imagine the town where Jesus told the story. It's the next morning. Let's take a little walk to the market and pick up the morning paper. Just like I suspected—take a look at the headline on the *Jerusalem Herald*. "Hundreds Helped Overnight—the Example of One." The stories are numerous: Between the hours of 3:00 p.m. and sunset, a wave of humanitarianism swept across the region in unprecedented numbers. Several men in dressy work clothes were seen helping a farmer get his ox out of the ditch. A poor widow who was about to be evicted from her home received enough money to pay the rent for a whole year. The children in the orphanage for the blind had a great night because some teenagers came by to read them some exciting stories. And a thief turned himself in along with the money he had stolen from a man he said he robbed on the road to Jericho. Cool, huh? I forgot to mention that one of the thieves was also in the crowd listening to Jesus that day and got his locked heart picked by the one who can work like a thief in the night.

D E L V E

How do you think you would have responded to those deacons who wanted to fire me?

_____

_____

In what way have you seen your church or the church in general react negatively to someone who is on fire for God's glory?

_____

_____

_____

Describe the way you saw the hand of God working in that situation.

_____

_____

_____

Start now and develop a list of people in your church or life who need to have God pick their locked hearts. Pray that the hearts of these people will be unlocked so they can bring healing to others who are hurting.

_____

_____

_____

*Jesus, today I pray for those who have locked hearts.
Pick them with your power and fling them open to
become tender and kind toward others. Jesus, the
church is filled with personal agendas and prejudices.
Please turn our hearts toward you. Amen.*

28

Rewards

I thank my God upon every remembrance of you.

Philippians 1:3

Let's keep our imagination going and scan that *Jerusalem Herald* again. There is one more story I want us to check out. It only received back-page coverage, but it is important to Jesus. Do you see it? It's the small story at the bottom, the one titled, "The Healer and the Hurt Reunited." Let's read it together.

> City Council members have been working frantically to increase security on the road from Jerusalem to Jericho. The stretch of winding, hilly terrain has given our community more than ten sad stories in the past year. Today one of those heartbreaking stories took a turn for the good.
>
> Famed Rabbi Jesus of Nazareth broke the story about the bloody altercation with a traveler and the thugs our city

leaders have been trying to bring to justice. After enduring the typical "pass by" and "pass on" by our religious leaders, the traveler got a lift from an unlikely helper. A Samaritan, who had probably taken a few Jewish classes on first aid, came to his rescue.

The two were reunited yesterday in what chief administrators are calling "a calibrated artistic ploy to hypnotize our citizens to buy into Jesus's stump speech to increase his following." In an emotional display, the Jewish traveler was seen actually touching and embracing the Samaritan. An anonymous observer on the ground stated, "Yeah, it was tough to watch. But given the situation with the Samaritan helping him and all, I guess it was okay for them to embrace." None of the individuals involved were available for comment.

The world may never get the story right. Even Jesus said there will be many who miss the point altogether due to their absorption into other interests and goals. But can I tell you who will not miss the point? You want to know who will definitely get the story straight? The guy hobbling up that hill to give a hug to that hurt healer, that's who!

Have you ever heard or seen a Jewish person express his or her gratitude? It's a beautiful thing. It's a loud, wet-kiss, face-hugging, celebration of joy. The Samaritan never saw it coming, but he certainly could hear it coming his way. Here's how it happened:

The recovering traveler catches a glimpse of the Samaritan on the ridge when Jesus points toward him. While the rest of the crowd stands there mesmerized by Jesus's storytelling ability, he gets busy hiking up that ridge. As soon as the word *likewise* leaves the lips of Jesus, shouts of joy come from the mouth of the victim.

"Mr. Samaritan! Oh, Mr. Samaritan, my good man, don't leave! Don't go anywhere. I'm coming up to see you, Mr. Samaritan!" shouts the bandaged man.

Already overcome with the elation of getting a nod from God, the Samaritan braces himself on the haystack. *Who in the world is this guy who's calling out to me?* he thinks. It isn't a terrible distance down the hill, but from what the Samaritan can tell, the guy with the crutches isn't going to make it too far up.

Louder now and rising above the murmurs of the inquisitive crowd, the voice of the victim bellows, "It was you! It was you! You, my dear Samaritan, are the one to whom I owe my life!"

Could it be? thinks the Samaritan. His heart leaps with wonder. "Is it you, dear traveler? Is it you?" shouts back the Samaritan.

"Yes! Oh yes, and I will ever be your debtor!" comes the reply. Amazed, the Samaritan races down to meet him.

The rescued reunited with the rescuer. Their embrace is careful, but their emotions are wild as the two men hug. Cheek kisses are being tossed all over the place in a flurry of thankfulness. There is no wall of prejudice that can withstand the tsunami of gratitude. Soaked from the wave of appreciation, the men hold each other by the shoulders, looking at each other from head to toe.

The Samaritan speaks first, "You are okay, my friend?"

"Yes, thanks to you," replies the Jew.

You may be thinking right about now that I have a wild imagination. Some people dismiss my thoughts as pie-in-the-sky dreaming. Sure, I have taken some creative liberty here, but I was able to come up with the idea out of my own experiences. When hurt healers touch your life, it marks you, and you want to seek them out to bless them for blessing you. Just like those mentioned in the *Jerusalem Herald* two thousand years ago, my life has also been altered by those who dared to be hurt healers. I am who I am today because hurt healers along my journey took the time to pause, prove, and pay.

I have discovered that it is a very uplifting experience to remember hurt healers and what they have done for you in the past. Take a moment, go grab a cup of coffee or iced beverage, get a pen and paper, and jot down a few of them. I'm thinking about Scott Christmas, who led me in the sinner's prayer that cold night in February. Lefus and Pat Hughes helped me move out of my van and into their house for a short but needed season. Steve Whitcomb opened his heart and his home to this former ghetto thief, rent-free with groceries included. Rob Carroll employed me with odd jobs when I couldn't get a job anywhere else because of my past record.

When hurt healers touch your life, you want to seek them out to bless them for blessing you.

My minister friend, Tommy Mallard, befriended and invested time in me and gave me an awesome example to follow and room to stumble through those early days of my Christian life. A senior adult couple, Murray and Anne Ashwell, took the time every Friday night to mentor my wife and me. We were blessed to sit at their precious feet and glean from their years of walking with God. The list could go on and on.

These treasured hurt healers poured oil and wine all over my healing wounds and made me a better person because of it. Bottom line, we are no more than what God gifts us to become and what we have had the privilege to gain from the investments of others.

I also have many hurt healers who pour oil and wine into my life currently. My mind immediately goes to all the people who email, send Facebook messages, or call and give me an encouraging word. You guys have dumped gallons of oil and wine into my heart. I'm also thinking of all the music artist friends I have: Stephen Curtis Chapman, Eddie Carswell,

TobyMac, Mark Hall—there are too many to mention. Through their friendships and life experiences they have helped me recover from many of the thief's attacks.

Louie Giglio is a famed and task-saturated preacher. Yet he has taken the time to meet with me and let me ask questions about things that troubled me deeply. He has a way of making you understand how great that oil and wine is because it is from a great and glorious God.

My pastor, Dr. Johnny Hunt, has been one of the most faithful preachers I know to consistently and compassionately preach the gospel of God's love and forgiveness. He has also been the dad to me that I always wanted. We don't fish or do birthdays together; he just extends a father's touch toward me. He gave me a card one day and in it wrote, "I love you like a son." That card was oily, slick with the love of God being poured out by a pastor, friend, and father figure. I can't count how many times I've hugged that man's neck in gratitude.

The strongest hurt healer I have in my life today is my sweet wife, Tammy. You know that the person married to me must have bottomless bowls of oil and wine to live with me. She does. She always puts her own comfort on pause and proves her compassion by daily paying what it takes to nurture our children, keep our home, and administrate in our ministry, all the while loving and respecting me. She is truly a gift from God.

In the last four years, I have traveled and preached to over two million people and have seen hundreds of thousands of them respond to Jesus by faith and repentance. I have been a voice for the voiceless orphans and helped get sponsors to provide help for thousands of them. None of this could have happened if it were not for those who have been hurt healers in my life. I have wept over the healing all of these people brought into my life, and I have asked the Lord to let them join me on my reward day in heaven so that I can share my prize with them. And after I have rubbed, kissed,

202

and held the reward high for all of the saints to see, it will be placed at the feet of the ultimate hurt healer, Christ Jesus the Lord!

At this moment, however, while Jesus is proliferating this story of extravagant love, forgiveness, and gratitude, there are no rewards around the feet of Jesus. He is still standing there at the bottom of that hill. Dirt and sweat cover his feet from standing there in the hot sun telling his story. He does, however, have a reward, and it is watching those two guys on the side of that mound clapping, hugging, kissing, and weeping. One of his commandments had been lived out by a "least likely to succeed" guy, and by the looks on the faces of the so-called spiritually elite watching the celebration, he has confounded the wise. But there is no surprise in Jesus's mind. He knows the powerful connection that happens between people when the cost is paid so that compassion and caring heals the heart of someone who is hurting.

Watching the reunion between the hurting and the healer, Jesus's smile widens and tears spill from his compassionate eyes as both his hands are raised in praise to God the Father. It's a picture of the reunion he will have one day with those who are hurting from Satan's attacks but will be rescued by his love and forgiveness through the price he is joyfully willing to pay at the cross.

D E L V E

Take a few minutes and recall the people who have invested in you and taken time to be hurt healers in your life. Write their names down.

_____

_____

_____

Think about and articulate specifically what kind of impact they have had on you.

_____

_____

_____

Take some time today and email them or write them a letter simply thanking them for their investment in your life.

_____

_____

_____

Whose life are you currently investing in as a hurt healer? Ask God to lead you to someone this week who could benefit from your investment in them.

_____

_____

_____

My great God, I thank you today for the hurt healers whom you have used in my life. I am no more today than what you have gifted me to be and what I have become because of the investments others have made in my life. I thank you for them. I call them out to you by name, and I pray that you will favor them for the favor they have shown to me. Amen.

29

Think about It

And God said to Moses, "I AM WHO I AM."

Exodus 3:14

What a story, huh? I am so thrilled you took the time to make this journey with me. I get jazzed thinking about the hope and healing that is going to wash all over the hearts of your friends, classmates, coworkers, and family members because you chose to be a hurt healer. Your life of pausing and paying will be proof that God is great.

Remember, though, that being a hurt healer is not just about doing random acts of kindness. Rather it's about doing Deliberate Divine Deeds. A Divine Deed has within its DNA the gospel of Jesus Christ. A hurt healer mends both wounds on the skin and the wounds caused by sin. Hurt healers are not merely humanitarians; they are evangelistic humanitarians. In this chapter I want to share with you one more thought and a story to help you fully understand why it is so essential for a hurt healer to have this evangelistic emphasis.

One of the most influential books I have read since becoming a Christian is *I Am Not but I Know I Am* by Louie Giglio. I received a copy of the book as a gift. When I opened it, I was surprised to see Louie had signed it for me. "To Tony—you have a great role in His story." I was encouraged, and after reading it I was inspired. It is a must-read for every human being. I want to share a couple of snippets from that book that have helped shape a lot of my evangelistic emphasis as a hurt healer.

Hurt healers are not merely humanitarians; they are evangelistic humanitarians.

The short summary of the book is that life is about two stories: the story of you, which is tiny and short, and the story of God, which is enormous and eternal. In the book Louie makes the case for us to exchange being preoccupied with living for our story and trying to make it bigger, to living in a supporting role of the grand story of God. He says something that is as weighty as any truth that has come out of the councils throughout church history that have helped shape and define Christianity as we know it. Giglio writes,

> If we don't get the two stories straight, everything else in our lives will be out of sync. We'll spend our days trying to hijack the story of God, turning it into the story of us. Inverting reality, we'll live every day as though life is all about you and me. We will live as though life is our one-act play and history is our story, as though creation is our habitation alone, existence our playground and God our servant. (That is if we decide we need him at all.) We will throw every ounce of our energy into the fragmented and fleeting story of us. Calling the shots ourselves, me-centered thinking will dictate every move we make and how we feel. And in the end, when the last clap is clapped for our tiny tale, our story will fade to black, a pitiful return on our one-shot chance called life on earth.[1]

SHOWING JESUS

I have read that page over a hundred times. Louie's thoughts are a great backdrop for the hurt healer's life. It's a hurt healer's worldview, or should I say *storyview*?

Louie also makes a comment to an inquisitive police officer about his message to college students that resonates strongly with the Spirit of God in me. He tells the officer, "I am going to remind them that life is short and our time on earth is really brief. That's why we have to make sure our lives count for the stuff that lasts forever." You may have heard me repeat variations of this reply throughout this book and in my live messages. Those who know me have seen that since my conversion, I have always been wired to live the way Louie is suggesting. I nearly killed myself trying to live for the tiny story of Tony; now I am passionate about living in a supporting role in the unfolding, adventurous story of God.

When we think of the Good Samaritan, we think about humanitarianism, which has become a big focus for many young people in America. One of the core tasks of emerging young Christian humanitarians is cultural enhancement. Many will travel to different neighborhoods and foreign countries to do deeds that can alter the culture of hurting people. Schools get better, houses are built, and social care becomes more practiced. In the big picture, things on earth get better for people through cultural enhancement. The outstanding people working toward those changes are incredibly important and their work to make those changes should be praised, but is cultural enhancement alone going to fulfill the high calling of a hurt healer and tell the full story of God? I strongly suggest that this particular storyview that Louie expresses and I adhere to implies that it won't. Humanitarianism alone falls short of fully supporting the story of God because the plot of God's story climaxes with him advancing his kingdom. Track with me and keep reading.

More than once in my twenty-year journey of knowing Jesus, I have read through the Bible in a year. After I make it past the land allotments, genealogies, and some of the gross

Levitical law—including worship practices such as cutting the fatty lobe from a bull's kidney—I find it an enriching experience. Recently as I read through it, I wanted God to speak to me about this culture enhancement emphasis that is so prevalent today. As I read his unfolding story, he spoke clearly: "I love people; I proved that on the cross. But I'm not simply after cultural enhancement. My ultimate goal is my kingdom's advancement."

Humanitarianism alone falls short of fully supporting the story of God because the plot of God's story climaxes with him advancing his kingdom.

Do you see it? At first I didn't, but reading the Bible clearly revealed that the story of God advancing his kingdom is unfolding all around us. People, cities, and cultures are not center stage; God's kingdom is in the spotlight. Jesus highlighted this grand plot when he prayed, "Your kingdom come, your will be done, on earth as it is in heaven." Revelation, the sneak peek, early release book of coming attractions, supports this idea as well because it reveals the materialization of the advancement of the kingdom of God. He is all about advancing his kingdom.

Going into a community, city, or nation and doing things to make their world and culture a better place for people is good. I will go with you to feed the hungry and clothe the naked. Let's serve the least of these. But if that is all we do, then we could actually be extending the injustice they suffer by simply leaving them there to just get hungry and naked again.

There are those who say, "Let's intensify the humanitarian effort by creating an environment within their culture where they can be self-sustaining." Full-on, I'm with you! I will help you build the infrastructure for residual support. What I am saying, however, is that we need to remember that we are living in a sin-cursed world. I said earlier in the book that we *all* live in a bad neighborhood, and it's called

208   SHOWING JESUS

earth! Humanity will always suffer here. Yes, we should do all we can to stop the suffering. But hurt healers also ensure that people have made a connection with God so their lives can be abundant with purpose and eternally sustained in his coming kingdom.

Don't dismiss me as merely being one of those evacuation preachers who has no regard for the beauty of God's creation and his desire to redeem it. I love it, I love people, and believe me, I know he wants to redeem this earth. But he is not going to give it a makeover; he is going to make all things new. God is going to transform it altogether into a glorious kingdom where he rules and reigns in peace and love. But only those who have made peace with him through repentance of sin and faith in the finished work of his Son Jesus on the cross will get citizenship in that eternal kingdom. Therefore, we must share the gospel with non-Christians.

> **Hurt healers also ensure that people have made a connection with God so their lives can be abundant with purpose and eternally sustained in his coming kingdom.**

I guess I am suggesting that the WWJD factor may apply on this whole cultural enhancement emphasis too. Remember, the good can often be the enemy of the best. Enhancing culture is like merely doing a random act of kindness. It will help, but it's temporary. But when you go into a hungry neighborhood with the groceries *and* the gospel, you meet their temporary need and their eternal need as well. Now do you see it?

Here's how it breaks down in the daily routine of a hurt healer. Walk slowly along the road of your life. Watch out for those who have been ambushed by the fallout of our sin-cursed world. Tend to them and help mend their physical needs, and as you do, care for their spiritual needs as well with the oil and wine of God's gospel. It is not your responsibility to convince them to respond to Jesus. Your only task is to share; God does the saving. And mark it down, he will save, and he does so as we share the message—as we share the medicine. When we do that, the hurt people we know will get healing for their hurts here and gain access to live in a coming kingdom where hurts will be no more. Think about it.

I came across another story that illustrates and supports the wisdom behind being an evangelistic humanitarian. I read it in the book *The Eternity Portfolio*, by Alan Gotthardt. Alan is a choice example of what it means to be a pay-the-cost hurt healer. His book should be read by anyone who wants to more closely resemble Jesus because, as my pastor always says, "You are never more like Jesus than when you are giving." Gotthardt quotes an interesting twist on the Good Samaritan story that he heard from Gordon McDonald. "What if the Good Samaritan came along that road again the following week and found another man in the same condition? And then the same thing happened the following week? At some point, the Samaritan should ask himself, 'Should I continue paying for triage for the victims at the local inn, or should I invest in making this road a safer place?'"

I know sometimes it feels like we are forking out money and energy in a merry-go-round of exchanging bucks for blows. But be encouraged, hurt healer, because God has made an investment through the blood of his Son Jesus, and in so doing he has made a way for hurting hearts to gain access to a safer and better place called heaven. He will run off the cruel thief, and Satan will not be able to steal, kill, and destroy any longer. We will be shielded from all pain, harm, and wrong once and for all, safely within the pearly gates of his kingdom. As a guy who grew up in a ghetto, I'm looking forward to it. One day I'm leaving this old poverty-stricken, crime-infested, sinful world, and I'm moving into a beautiful place—the fullness of the presence of God.

What does it mean to you to be in a supporting role in the grand story of God?

_____

_____

_____

Articulate the difference between a person whose focus is on cultural enhancement and one whose focus is on kingdom advancement.

_____

_____

_____

In what ways are you currently and actively letting God use you to advance his kingdom?

_____

_____

_____

O God, thank you for my supporting role in your story. There is no ending to your epic, but I clearly see the glory of the story peaking when your kingdom comes on earth as it is in heaven. Lord, empower me to share your story with those who are hurting. Thank you for the hope that I will one day walk on streets of gold where thieves will never roam. Amen.

30

Christianity Rocks!

Oh, taste and see that the LORD is good; blessed is the man who trusts in Him!

Psalm 34:8

As I reflect back on the journey of writing this book, I recall some very special moments with my wife, Tammy. Each night after writing my chapters, I would read them to her to glean some insights and hope for her approval. She is such an encourager and a woman in touch with the heart of God. There were several moments that stand out in my mind. She did not like the opening sentence of chapter 1: "Christianity sucks." She just has this thing about the word *sucks*. It's gross, nasty, and not allowed to be said by my children because she says it's a "potty word."

I explained that I wasn't saying it, non-Christians were, but she still disapproved. We had quite a dispute over that word being in the book. I still look over my shoulder when

I'm typing those words, wondering if she is going to jump me, take over the keyboard, and censor that phrase.

She had many positive responses as well. One that rises above the others was the look on her face when I said that the *Jerusalem Herald* reported that one of the thieves who had ambushed the Jewish traveler actually turned himself in to authorities along with the money he had stolen from the man. I imagined that he was also in the crowd as Jesus was speaking and fell under deep conviction and repented of his wrongdoing. Tammy's face beamed with delight in the creative twist I injected, and her heart was pleased with the audacious dream that a moment like that could have happened. Perhaps when I get to heaven I will meet that robber and he'll smile and say, "Who would've thunk it?"

There are a lot of possibilities that could have happened in the context of that story. But the biggest possibility that captures my imagination is the one that I have about you and the response you will have to Jesus's story and the content of this book.

At the start of our journey together, I said I had high hopes that you would have a supernatural encounter with God and experience a life change that would cause the people who meet you to walk away saying, "This person gave me a good taste of Jesus, and now I have to say, 'blessed are those who trust in God!'" Hurting people need a better taste of Jesus—especially if David Kinnaman's and Gabe Lyons's report in *unChristian* is true that only 3 percent of young people in America have a favorable impression of Jesus as portrayed in the lives of evangelicals.

You also remember that I said I haven't always been a believer, nor did I grow up in church. This means that I share with outsiders some common negative ideas about Christianity. Most of these thoughts about Christians were false, and they faded away after my conversion into the Christian culture. There were other beliefs, however, that have not faded through my interactions with the Christian populace—ones that have proven to be shamefully true. One of the biggest shamefully true characteristic about Christians is the breakdown that happens between the God that we know and the God that we show. I hope that your time invested in reading this book has caused you to better know your God so you can better show him.

I hope that your time invested in reading this book has caused you to better know your God so you can better show him.

I so desire that you live differently than those who walked before you, who left their unfavorable impressions of Jesus in their wake. Live the life of a hurt healer so loudly and so radically that it actually gets news and media coverage. How cool would that be? Could you imagine a modern-day revolt happening as individuals catch the heart of God for the people he came to die for and hurt healers rise up to the occasion by the millions? The headlines and cover stories would be dramatically different. Instead of them saying things like, "Abortion Clinic Bombed," "Christians against Everything," or another heartbreaking account detailing how we are ultra right-wing, religious bigots spewing hate all over the culture, they would be oil-and-wine-soaked stories of God's love and redemption exhibited through our lives. But if the news media never gets our story right or misses it altogether, so what? Our goal is to help the hearts of the hurting to clearly get the message. And we can if we dare to do Deliberate Divine Deeds to one person at a time.

I have a ton of stories about people who have decided to be hurt healers. I wish I could share them all because each of them is significant and beautiful. Here is one story about a group of people who morphed from random acts to Deliberate Divine Deeds and what that looked like in their small community.

One hot and humid Saturday, a group of hurt healers met at their church at noon. Their goal was to do a deed to someone in need that would leave that person with a favorable impression of Jesus. Their focus was on a section of interstate that cut through the south side of their small town. Thousands of vehicles raced along that strip of road, and inevitably a motorist could be found broken down. This band of hurt healers set out to rescue any they found during the hottest part of the day.

They did a quick inventory to make sure they had all they needed to assist the travelers: a van to get to them, an envelope filled with plenty of cash that they had raised through various fund-raisers, a lawn chair, a cooler filled with cold drinks, two big peacock-feather fans, a cell phone, and a list of every business that dealt with automobiles within a five-mile radius of the highway. They gathered in a small circle and cried out passionately to God, asking him to guide them and use them for his glory. Then off they went.

Could you imagine a modern-day revolt happening as individuals catch the heart of God for the people he came to die for and hurt healers rise up to the occasion by the millions?

Within minutes they came across their first stranded motorist. He had two blown-out tires. The group pulled up next to him and filed out of the van like a Special Forces team on a recon mission. One of the young men introduced himself, "Hello, I'm Bradly. What's your name?"

"Carl," came the grumpy reply.

"How long have you been stranded, Carl?" asked Bradly.

"I've been here for over an hour roasting in this blistering heat with my hood up hoping someone would stop," Carl said, with a tone of desperation and disappointment.

Bradly chimed in, "Well, that's about to change for you, Mr. Carl." As they were talking, the rest of the group of seven went straight to work. Wil checked out the tires while Christy looked over her telephone list to find a company that could do roadside tire repairs. Meanwhile, Joy and Anna set up the lawn chair behind Mr. Carl while Hudson and Carter grabbed the cooler of drinks and the fans.

"Please have a seat, Mr. Carl," said Joy. He settled into the comfy recliner with Hudson and Bradly's help. Mr. Carl was well into his seventies, and the heat had taken its toll on his ability to stand up any longer. Once seated, he was immediately met with a refreshing burst of wind as Carter started waving the colorful peacock-feather fan up and down next to his sweaty brow.

Hudson opened the ice chest and asked, "What would you like to drink, Mr. Carl? We have sweet iced tea, Coke, a few diet drinks, and some root beer."

"Well, I don't really know," Mr. Carl started to say but didn't get to finish as Joy broke in with exuberant hospitality.

"Mr. Carl, this is not the time to be shy. It's hot out here, and if I were you I'd get one of those root beers. They're delicious."

Mr. Carl nodded, and Hudson quickly handed it over. Just then the tire service truck rolled up. After a very brief greeting, Christy instructed the repairman to do whatever it took to get the car fixed and he would be paid in cash on the spot. He started working immediately.

"Have you eaten lunch, Carl?" asked Wil.

"No, I haven't."

"What would you like?" asked Carter.

"Well, I don't . . . ," he stuttered.

Anna interjected, "There you go again. You're so cute. Why not just tell us what you like so we can go get it for you? I bet you like Wendy's and I can tell by your smile that you like their Frosty."

"Sure, but I don't want to impose," replied Carl. At that, Wil and Carter dashed off to Wendy's. Fifteen minutes later Carl had eaten a cheeseburger and was dipping his French fries in his Frosty while sitting in a recliner, cooled by undulating peacock feathers, watching his truck get a new set of tires. He was thinking, *Who in the world are these people?*

After the tire repairman was paid four hundred dollars, Bradly spoke up, "Mr. Carl, you're set to go. But before you leave we would like to tell you that we are Christians. And two thousand years ago on a cross, Jesus Christ told you that he loves you by paying the debt for your sins, which can be forgiven through repentance and faith in him. Today Jesus wanted to remind you that he has never stopped loving you. Here is our contact information, and if you want to learn more about Jesus we would love to help you with that. Have a great day, Mr. Carl."

Does this story sound a little over the top? No more over the top than a Samaritan helping a Jew by treating his wounds and giving him unlimited access to his credit card in addition to paying two days' wages. I bet you are also dying to ask if Mr. Carl ever accepted Christ. Well, let's not worry right now about whether Mr. Carl got saved, converted, born again, or any other word you want to use for someone getting swallowed up by God's forgiveness and grace. Instead, I've got a question for you. Do you think Mr. Carl drove away and screamed an obnoxious "Christianity sucks!" out of his window? I doubt it. I'm thinking that as he drove up the road still cooled from the fanning, burping on that mouthwatering burger, swigging down the last sip of that delicious root beer, all the while listening to the hum of his brand new tires race up the interstate, he's declaring, "Christianity rocks!"

And for all the naysayers who claim that people get offended when we do that because they think the only reason we took care of their problem is because we wanted to share Jesus with them, let me say, "I rebuke that thought in the name of Jesus and command that it go back to hell from which it came." Don't ever listen to those naysayers. Without even realizing it, they are being used by Satan to ambush and attack us to keep us from sharing the gospel and being hurt healers.

In over seventeen years of helping people, I have never—let me make myself clear here—never, never, never, never, ever had someone get mad at me or offended by me for sharing the gospel as I paid their rent, fixed their car, brought them a bag of groceries, took care of their medical bills, or served their needs. *Never!* One might tomorrow, but the way I look at it, that's one in seventeen years. That is an incredible service record.

⁓

I have one last question for you. Would you pray for me? You can stay informed about my family and ministry by tracking with me on Twitter @tonynolanlive, on Facebook at www.facebook.com/enjoyingjesus, or on my website www.tonynolan.org. I could use your strong prayer support. Why? Because *they* are calling. *They* haven't been silent since I realized they were out there some twenty years ago when I got saved. They have been crying out to you as well.

My mind is constantly haunted with the image of them lying in the intersection of life all withered up and half dead. I've told you how I am often overwhelmed by their stories of great burden. But today I have a sense of hope swelling up within me because I now have another image in my mind. It's of you, a hurt healer instead of a hurtful heretic, coming to their rescue.

Thank you for tuning in and keeping them on your radar. Go in God's power. Your reward will be great.

D E L V E

In what ways has this book helped you better know your God so you can better show your God?

_____

_____

_____

Invite four or five of your friends over for pizza this week. Tell them what a Deliberate Divine Deed is and read to them the story of the group of people who helped the guy whose truck had broken down. Now dare—that's right, I said dare—your friends to join you in doing something just like that within a week.

_____

_____

_____

Once you are done with the Divine Deed you and your friends planned, write out what happened. What did you feel as you did it? How did the person who received the help respond to you?

_____

_____

_____

Plan another Deliberate Divine Deed, and know I'm over here in my corner of the world doing the same—giving people a taste of Jesus so they can say he is good and blessed are those who trust in God.

_____

_____

_____

Sweet Lord Jesus, thank you for being the ultimate example of what it means to be a hurt healer. I make it my lifelong ambition to follow you. Help me to do this so others may know you and say along with me, "The Lord is good!" Amen.

Notes

Chapter 1: Know Show

1. David Kinnaman and Gabe Lyons, *unChristian* (Grand Rapids: Baker, 2007), 25.

Chapter 11: Focus!

1. Walter A. Elwell, ed., *Evangelical Dictionary of Theology* (Grand Rapids: Baker, 1984), 1118.

Chapter 25: Thumbs-Up!

1. Babbie Mason, "Show Me How to Love," *Carry On*, Word, B0006ULQ7A, audio CD, 1988.

Chapter 29: Think about It

1. Louie Giglio, *I Am Not but I Know I Am* (Sisters, OR: Multnomah, 2005), 13.

Tony Nolan is an author and sought-after speaker who recently served as tour pastor and Gospel communicator for the Casting Crowns Lifesong tour and Winter Jam, the largest Christian concert tour in America. He speaks to more than 800,000 people at more than 100 events a year, bringing the love of Jesus to a hurting world. While he is often on the road, his permanent residence is in Georgia.

Connect with Tony

 facebook.com/EnjoyingJesus

 twitter.com/tonynolanlive

 tonynolan.org

Tony Nolan's Resources

E-NEWSLETTER
Sign up online to get the latest news and updates from Tony.

TONY'S MESSAGES
Subscribe to Tony's sermon podcast online via iTunes.

FAITH FUEL
Tony shares how small steps of faith can set you on an adventurous journey with God.

SCARED OR PREPARED
This DVD contains a life-changing message Tony preached on tour across America. God has used it to help 73,000 people embrace his love!

visit tonynolan.org